# Advanced Memory Palaces

Joe Reddington

**Abstract**

People into memory techniques and Computer Science both attack the same question: how do I structure this information in the most effective way? Every traditional memory technique has a matching one in Computer Science, but the reverse isn't true: in this book I show how a set of techniques created for computers can be used can be used for long-term personal memory.

This book is about memory palaces. It is not about speed memorising digits for memory competitions, it is about holding a massive amount of structured information in your head and making sure it is usable. It should be the second book you read on memory; I have written for people who've already had an introduction to the field and found simple methods useful.

# Acknowledgements

Thank you to Kat, who gave me the space and time to write this book and to Leo and Nova for giving me reasons to write it.

Thank you to Adrian and Elizabeth who got me to think in terms of data-structures and to Seb for being part of the conversations that later became this book.

Thank you to my beta-readers: Lyle, Ali and Imogen, my cover artist Michelle, Sarah Kuklewicz, my expert reader John Holden, and a small army of people who proofread, answered questions on Facebook and generally provided a supporting chorus. This book is yours.

# Contents

# Chapter 1

# Introduction

This should be the second book you read on memory techniques.

It doesn't matter which other book you read first, but you'll find it easier if you've had some practice of both using memory techniques well and discovering their limitations.

Between 2003 and 2014, I was a Computer Science researcher at a string of universities. People into memory techniques and people into Computer Science both attack the same question: how do I structure this information in the most effective way? Every technique in memory has a matching one in Computer Science, but the reverse isn't true: in this book I show how a set of techniques created for computers can be used for long-term personal memory.

This book guides you through a series of examples that show how insights from Computer Science can be used to refine existing memory techniques and create brand new ones. It also covers, in detail, the construction and maintenance of an effective memory palace.

This chapter is a guide to my basic assumptions and beliefs, covers why a memory palace is vital for long-term storage and gives a list of the contributions that the book makes. It goes on to give an overview of the rest of the book and defines the notation that I use.

## 1.1 Setting the scene

A good first chapter makes the underlying beliefs of the author obvious so that the reader can see if there is anything to violently disagree with. Here are the four beliefs that underpin this work.

### 1.1.1 All memories fade

All memories fade. Some last longer than others but it's hard to say which ones will last. The memory techniques in this book and others can extend the lifespan of a memory from minutes to months, but it will still fade eventually.[1]

However, memories don't suddenly vanish. Instead, they slowly become less detailed, which means that a good way to stop the information from disappearing is to regularly review it. This isn't a novel concept; it's the whole concept of revision before an exam.

---

[1]Competitive memorists use this to their advantage by carefully letting the last event's information fade before the next one, see [O'Brien, 2016] for an account of the process.

If you use some memory techniques to remember information, then reviewing them periodically will extend your period of reliable recall from months to decades.

To review the memories, you need to know what memories you have. To know what memories you have, you are going to need a list. Once you have a list, you may as well memorise that as well.

For example, the first five items on my list of 'things I have memorised' goes like this:

1. The Rudyard Kipling poem If.

2. The set of 52 keywords words in the Java programming language.

3. A set of nice memories.

4. Chapter and verse information for some literary passages.

5. The set of countries in OPEC.

With this list, I can review literally everything I've ever committed to memory. By reviewing your list regularly, you find you can rely on everything you've stored being there when you might need it. Chapter 9 goes into the review process in detail.

That list of 'things I have memorised' is your memory palace. The purpose of the memory palace is to make it possible to review your memories. Nothing else. A memory palace makes it no easier to access the memories you've stored,[2] but, properly maintained, it does mean that those memories will be clear and reliable.

[2]Indeed, it makes it slightly harder to store them.

**DEFINITION 1** *A* memory palace *is a memorised list of different sets of information you have memorised.*

This definition might be jarring. We naturally want to think of a memory palace as a towering mental structure, built up of the most lovely places we can imagine, full of strange and vivid imagery that encodes tremendous amounts of data. In that context 'a list of things you have memorised' seems rather weak.

This book will demonstrate that the towering mental structure really is a list (Chapter 4) and it really is full of strange and vivid imagery (Chapter 2). However, that isn't the only way of constructing a memory palace and so the definition is broad enough to include different approaches and simple enough that it's clear what the real purpose is: to aid reviewing.

### 1.1.2 No filler

The second core belief of this book is: write what you know.

There is almost nothing in this book on the history of memory techniques.[3] Nor is there anything on the brain.[4] Literally no words start with 'neuro'. I know nothing about brain chemistry and shouldn't be telling other people about it. The contributions of this book are ones that I am sure of and have experience with.

---

[3]It would be impossible to do a better job than [Yates, 1992].

[4]Sometimes I cite a study when making a general point, but that will be from behavioural studies rather than anything involving an MRI machine.

### 1.1.3 Paper beats rock

The third core belief of this book is: Computer Science has better tools.

In the late 80s BC, an unknown author wrote Rhetorica Ad Herennium.[5] It has a long section on memory techniques, which simply and elegantly lays out almost all of the methods used by people interested in memory techniques today.

This is breathtaking because in the *21 centuries* since then, hundreds of books have been published on memory[6] and they have collectively managed to add little to the set of techniques or even refine the methods. The sole innovation is that methods for memorising long series of numbers have been created, such as the Major System, the Dominic System, and the Person-Action-Object System.

Many of the books are useful as enjoyable introductions and guides [Brown, 2007, Lorayne, 1958], autobiographies [O'Brien, 2016, Foer, 2012], or guides for specialist training [Yousaf, 2006, Marbas and Pelley, 2002]; but they don't tend to add anything new from a technical perspective, nor do they place the methods within a framework that allows users to reason about the best approach.

When I started writing this book I was a researcher in theoretical Computer Science. I spent my days looking at the design of programming languages and teaching undergraduates about data-structures. I was marinated in

[5] I use the translation by [Caplan and Winterbottom, 2016].

[6] Almost all of them have a picture of a brain on the cover.

a culture of thinking deeply about effective and efficient storage of information.

Existing in this culture made it hard not to see the deep parallels between personal memory techniques and the structures used in everyday programming.

Everything I learned about memory techniques fit naturally into my Computer Science framework, and I became fascinated by the parallels between memory techniques and my day job. The more I looked into the field, the more it became clear that there were ideas and techniques that were used in Computer Science that could be immediately and effectively used for people to significantly improve their storage of, and importantly, their access to information.

On top of this, it was clear that a Computer Science approach represented a more critical way of thinking about the structures that memorists already used. For example, an undergraduate course on Computer Science will include two particular data-structures: linked lists and arrays. A linked list behaves almost exactly like something memorists call the *Chain Method* and an array can be made to work exactly like something memorists call the *Method of Loci.* Students would be expected to be able to compare and contrast these and maybe ten or fifteen other data-structures. They would be expected to choose appropriate ones for any given situation and be able to justify that choice. By contrast, most memory books would discuss the equivalent structures entirely separately, and, in general, present the Chain Method as a beginner's technique and the Method of Loci as an advanced one.

I'll grant that the Method of Loci is harder to learn, but that doesn't mean it's more effective: it's harder for most English speakers to learn Thai than Spanish, but it would be foolish to assume that Thai is always more useful.

The Computer Science community is much younger than the memory one, but it is vastly larger, and is driven by a great deal of money. Over the decades it has produced, argued about, refined, and codified thousands of ways of storing information. Most importantly it has worked out which ones are best in which situations. The guiding principle this book uses is: what if Computer Scientists designed and structured a memory palace?

### 1.1.4 This isn't going to help you win a memory tournament

This book isn't going to help you become a memory world champion. There are two reasons. Firstly, it's not my goal: this is a book about high-quality long term recall of structured information rather that fast memorisation of temporary information.

The second reason is that competitive memory events are designed to test a particular memory technique: the Method of Loci.

If you asked a set of randomly chosen people what would be a good event to have in a memory competition you would be likely to get answers like:

- Watch a short film and then be asked questions about it.

- Read a book and then answer written questions about it.[7]
- Be taken blindfolded into a very complex crowded room, and given ten seconds to look at it before having to describe it in as much detail as possible.
- Be shown a picture and then have to draw it from memory.
- A spelling bee.

Events like this don't appear in the World Memory Championships. The World Memory Championships events boil down to 'How well can you use the Method of Loci?'. They include:

- Remember this list of playing cards and recite it back.
- Remember this list of numbers and recite it back.
- Remember this list of binary digits and recite it back.

The Method of Loci is talked about in detail in Chapter 4, but it's a small part of the overall landscape.

This book attempts to place the Method of Loci in its proper place - as a useful technique amongst many others rather than the magic hammer that it has been portrayed as for the last few decades. Notably, the highly influential [Lorayne, 1958], which was published some years before the Championships started, focuses on a number of

[7] We call this one 'an exam'.

quite different memory feats and is highly disdainful of the Method of Loci, dismissing it inside of a page.[8]

This is a good point to make a terminology note: this book uses the term 'memorist' to refer to the community of people familiar with memory methods as laid out in Rhetorica Ad Herennium and countless books since (generally in sentences like 'Memorists call this the Method of Loci but we can see that it's another instance of an array').

## 1.2 My goals for this book

The fundamental goal of this book is to deliver on its title: you will learn about memory palaces and they will be advanced. You will be able to construct a true memory palace: to have all of your information within reach, to be able to audit it, strengthen it, and build on it.

The second goal is to give people interested in memory the tools and insights that Computer Scientists have been using for decades. I want readers to ask themselves questions like:

- How often will I need this?
- Will I need to recite all of it, or will I be recalling individual parts?

[8] To be clear, Harry Lorayne was a magician performing a memory act. He's highly influential as a magician rather than in the popular memory literature. I strongly suspect that most of the good work done in personal memory techniques is done by the magic community who, quite reasonably, don't want to share their approach publicly.

- How large is the set of items?

- Will I have time to think for a second or does recall have to be instant?

- Am I organising memories I already have, or is everything entirely new?

- What other information might I need at the same time?

Most of all, I want readers to be able to pick a suitable structure (or multiple smaller ones) for every set of possible answers to the above questions.

## 1.3 Contributions

This book is written in a crowded field so I want to be clear about its unique contributions.

- Techniques within a framework

  This is the first book that places personal memory techniques in the data-structure framework of Computer Science. This makes it the first book to easily compare the techniques in terms of how fast structures are to make, how quickly they let you find information, how hard they are to work with and how easy they are to change.

- New Structures

Many memory books talk about linked lists or arrays,[9] but none talk about trees, classes, or skip lists. These 'new' structures are often useful in places where linked lists and arrays aren't and they are the biggest contribution from the view of a memory hobbyist.

- Putting structures together

  Because other memory books have few basic structures, the combinations of those structures are fairly boring. In this book you will see an array that contains classes that contain linked lists (Section 4.6); and you'll be able to make complex structures of your own that match the structure of the information you are trying to store.

- A review of my own memory palace

  I have made, looked after, and used a reasonably large[10] memory palace and I made many mistakes along the way. I'm going to tell you about the mistakes as often as I talk about the successes.

---

[9] Never with those words.

[10] I have no way of comparing to other people, so 'reasonably large' says more about the tug of war between my ego and my self-awareness than anything else.

## 1.4 The second book you read on memory techniques

Please read this book differently than books on basic techniques. In [Brown, 2007] Derren Brown says:

> Please try out the techniques as you are invited to, even if you have never thought about improving your memory. They really are fun, surprisingly and immensely useful, and it takes very little effort to play along as you read them. At the risk of over-stressing the point, if you merely read through them without applying yourself at all, they will seem only daft and unworkable; whereas if you do try them for yourself, the next pages could excitingly transform aspects of your life.

He's right to say that *for his book*. His book contains *exercises*.

However, this book contains examples, not exercises. They are here to interest you, point out factors you might not have considered, and give you ideas for your own systems. Some of them are *wrong* and I break down what makes them wrong. Sometimes the book will take you into a dead end before showing the you 'right' answer.

This book will only work when read by people who are already curious about memory techniques and who already believe in the value of the basics.

I want this to be your second memory book for several selfish reasons. One is that I'd rather have a few keen readers than a lot of bored ones. Another is that I really don't want to write two more introduction chapters in 'sales mode' telling you about the amazing powers you'll have. That's neither my style nor my talent, and it's a waste of your time to pad out the book.[11]

Those are both good reasons for making this the second book you read on memory, but the most honest reason is that I have doubts.

I don't have doubts about how good the material is: I would bet my house on that. I have doubts about the usefulness of large scale memory palaces in everyday life. There are parts of my memory palace that I use daily, but there are also parts that have never been useful, and parts that have only been useful for impressing people that, looking back, were not worth impressing. Certainly a well made memory palace would be great if I were approaching a large set of exams or worked as a surgeon, but I would feel like a fraud writing about the 'life changing effects of mastering your memory'.[12]

So, if you know that this is something you want, then I can give you the tools to make you great, and the cynicism and context to keep you human about it. But if you don't already want this, then you should find another book.

---

[11] I do let myself have a self indulgent last chapter, so there is *some* padding.

[12] I made this quote up, and I'm scared to search for it in case it turns out to be real.

## 1.5 Overview

This book has three distinct parts that guide you from an overview of the fundamentals, to steadily more complex examples, and finally to general discussion of the principles. I'm afraid that most of the content that one might think of as 'classic memory palace' ends up in the last third of the book.

### 1.5.1 Fundamentals

The first four chapters give a complete, but quick, introduction to personal memory techniques. You will find much of it familiar, but you should still read through: these chapters set out the principles and terminology that later parts build on.

- Chapter 2 covers ways to pick out keywords and create good links. It includes an outline of the Major System for storing numbers.

- Chapter 3 covers Linked Lists, which are fast to build, but slow to get information back out of; they are also fragile.

- Chapter 4 covers arrays, including the famous Method of Loci: arrays are the most common, and some of the most useful structures used by memorists.

### 1.5.2 New structures

The next part of the book covers new structures.

- Chapter 5 covers Classes, which are excellent for storing information about groups of similar objects.
- Chapter 6 covers Trees, which have many uses, particular in terms of quickly searching for information.
- Chapter 7 covers Karnaugh Maps, which work like a compressed decision tree.

This part contains the main contributions of the book to the field.

### 1.5.3 Beyond information

The last third of the book is a general discussion of memory palaces and their uses. It covers the overall design of a memory palace (Chapter 8) and keeping it in good shape (Chapter 9). Finally, Chapter 10 indulgently talks a lot about how the book was written and the sections I wanted but couldn't include.

## 1.6 How to read this book

This section gives some details on the naming and formatting conventions in this book, it also defines some of the basic terms that I use throughout.

### 1.6.1 Naming conventions

I have named the chapters after their Computer Science constructs because they are more general and more tightly defined than their traditional names. More practically:

there aren't traditional names for some of the structures and I didn't want to switch between styles.

The first use of an important term is generally done *in italics*, and will normally be followed by a more formal definition.

### 1.6.2 First definitions and notation

Our basic unit of memory is a *keyword.*[13]

**DEFINITION 2** *A* keyword *is a word, short phrase, physical object, or experience that captures data.*

A keyword[14] can be (and most often is) the name of a physical object ('dinosaur', 'latch'), a short phrase ("Onyx Gem"), or an everyday word or object. Many of these words encode other data: Section 4.7 shows how the spelling of "Onyx Gem" gives information about Scrabble words and Section 2.3 shows how 'latch' becomes '178'. In general, the keyword is 'the thing, or part of the thing, that you are trying to remember'. The amount of information a keyword gives you can vary: I use five keywords to remember my partner's mobile phone number, but only one to recall all the two letter words in Scrabble that include an 'e'.

[13]Sometimes I might write 'key phrase', or 'key image' when the sentence would otherwise be unwieldy.

[14]I use the word in the information retrieval sense, rather than in the programming sense that computer scientists may naturally think of. When writing the book I also considered 'tag', 'index', and 'item' so feel free to pick one of those if you like it more.

All memory techniques are, at their most basic, ways of linking one keyword to another. I use the notation 'A $\rightarrow$ B' to show that the keywords A and B are linked. This link is normally in the form of a linking image, but Chapter 4 will show some other ways of linking two keywords.

**DEFINITION 3** *Two keywords are* linked *if one keyword makes you think of another. We call the thoughts you have as you move from one to the other the* link.

The book shows different ways of arranging those links, so you may see diagrams that look like this

$$A \rightarrow B \rightarrow C \rightarrow D \rightarrow E$$

or even:

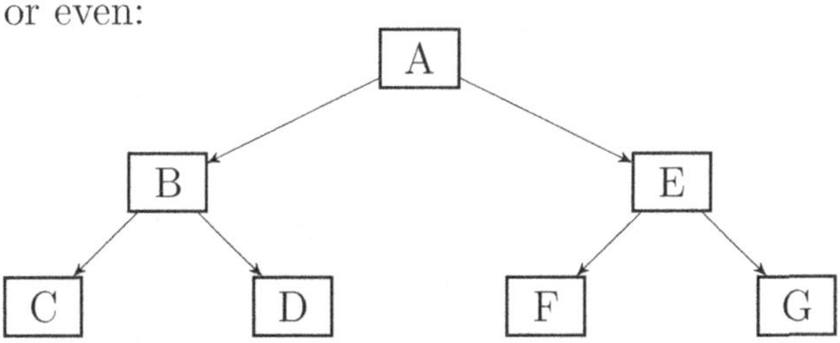


It's important to note that some keywords don't need new links because you already have them. I will always remember that the 2012 Olympics were in London because I was living there, and will always remember various historical facts or notes because they happened to be in a film I watched or a computer game I played. Such natural links get used a lot in this book and for them I use the notation:

$$A \Longrightarrow B$$

We all find different bits of information easier or harder to remember. I may have the pair of links:

$$\text{Declaration of independence} \rightarrow 1776$$

$$\text{Star Wars release date} \Longrightarrow 1977$$

but many people would have a natural link where I had an artificial link and vice versa.

### 1.6.3 Examples in the book

There are many examples in the rest of the book, both of structures and of links. Descriptions of linking images appear in boxes outside of the main text. The example below shows a linking image I use to connect the keyword 'Tyrannosaurus Rex' to the keyword 'Osborn'.[15]

| Tyrannosaurus Rex $\rightarrow$ Osborn |
|---|
| I see the T-Rex chase scene from Jurassic Park, except that the car is occupied by Norman Osborn, also known as Spider-Man's arch-enemy Green Goblin. Osborn is throwing his trademark pumpkin bombs at the dinosaur, who is gobbling ('Goblin') them up like a dog getting thrown treats as he gets closer and closer to the truck... |

These link descriptions are meant to show how I link the images: it's unlikely that they will work for anyone

[15]Henry Fairfield Osborn is credited with identifying the Tyrannosaurus Rex.

else (the above linking image only works if you have seen two specific films: *Jurassic Park (1993)* and *Spiderman (2002)*).

# Chapter 2

# Types

This chapter is about the fundamental building block of memory techniques: how to pick two keywords and how to link them together strongly.

This chapter uses three examples: one to show how a linking image is made, one to show several ways that you can access keywords, and one to demonstrate the use of the Major System converting numbers to keywords.

## 2.1 Which key?

Consider you have moved into a flat and have been given a set of keys of different colours. The green key is for the back door, the yellow key is for the front door and you never find out what the blue key is for.[1]

You want to make sure you always use the right key for the right door. What's the best way to do this?

[1]This example is indeed from my own life.

First, simplify the problem as far as possible. It's not "Which key is for which door?", it's "I want to think 'Yellow' when I see the front door".

I did it by imagining the door was covered in custard. I imagined An enormous amount of custard was pouring out of the crack at the top and around the sides, like the whole house was full to bursting with it. I could see dark yellow through the small windows and feel the sticky horribleness[2] when I touched it. I imagined the sharp sweet smell filling the landing. Once I'd done that, I never forgot which key was which.

You'll note that I didn't connect 'this door' and 'yellow'. I connected 'this door' and 'custard': I felt sure that I wasn't going say "I'm remembering custard, but I don't know which of the yellow, blue, or green keys I meant...".

This is the structure I used:

$$\text{the door} \rightarrow \text{custard} \Longrightarrow \text{yellow key}$$

Using an image to link two keywords is the basic building block of almost all memory techniques.

Making these images is a skill. You get better with practice, but there are some helpful guidelines:

1. The stranger the image is, the more likely you are to remember it (psychologists call this the Bizarreness Effect.[3]). Make it violent or obscene: if you are happy to tell people what the image is, then it's probably not strange enough.

[2]I am not, as it happens, fond of custard.

[3]For more context, see work by [Einstein and McDaniel, 1987, McDaniel et al., 1995, Riefer and Rouder, 1992].

2. I linked two solid objects: custard and a particular door. Abstract concepts (dates, numbers, etc) need to be changed into physical ones for this to work.

3. I involved all five senses to create the image. The more senses you imagine, the better it will lock in.

4. The direction of the link is important: I don't think of that door whenever I see custard; I think of custard whenever I see that door.[4]

5. The image should be *fun*, you should delight in thinking about the comedy of it, the strangeness.

Reading lots of different memory books helps you get better: the more examples of other people's images you find, the more ideas you'll have for your own. This is why I've used a lot of my own images in this book.

Keep *redundancy* in mind when making your image detailed. Memories generally don't vanish, but they do become less detailed. When I tell you to think about a link as completely as possible, to hear the sounds and smell the smells, I'm doing it not only to link the keywords, but also to make the link safer. For example, if you have a link in your memory structure that involves a giant dog attacking an aircraft carrier, then you don't *need* to imagine the discolouring you can see on the dog's teeth as it crunches though the deck or see the panic in the control tower, or hear the creaking of metal under stress, but all of those extra details will give you a few more weeks or months before you need to review the memory

[4]This is talked about properly in Section 3.1.1.

again because those are the details that will disappear first.

## 2.2 PIN code

Consider that the Halifax Bank has given you a new PIN code of 5160 for your new bank card and you dutifully want to memorise it. The link you want to make is:

$$\text{Halifax} \rightarrow 5160$$

Here's some potential images for the keyword '5160':

- A Star Wars Stormtrooper firing wildly into a bar, but every shot glances off some reflective surface and slams into the dartboard hitting the top score (there's a social group named the '51st legion' for people who enjoy dressing up as Star Wars characters and the top score for a single throw in darts is 60).
- A tiny 2d demon (sulfur's atomic number is 16, and we associate brimstone with demons), trapped inside the images on a £50 banknote, giving us 5(16)0.
- An alien (Area 51) being interviewed on the US show *60 minutes.*
- Doc Hudson of the Pixar film *Cars* (whose racing number is 51) is racing against Nick Cage in his *Gone in 60 seconds* persona.

- You receive a DVD copy of the film *51st State*, but for some reason the disk is shaped in the form of an equilateral triangle (so all the interior angles are exactly 60 degrees) and are struggling to find a DVD player that will work.

This process is sometimes called 'chunking': using existing natural links to account for several digits at a time. The first three examples were off the top of my head, the second two I looked up on Wikipedia (Wikipedia has a separate page for most of the natural numbers below 100 so it's a rich source of good images: see Figure 2.2 for example).

There are two things I'd like you to take from this example:

1. You already have a large set of natural links between numbers and images in your head and part of the skill in remembering short sequences like this is to quickly pick out the parts that have meaning to you.

2. It's okay to use sources like Google and Wikipedia to create the image as long as you don't need them to recall it.

To complete the example, I'm going to take the first idea on the list of possible images for the keyword '5160' and link it to the Halifax keyword.

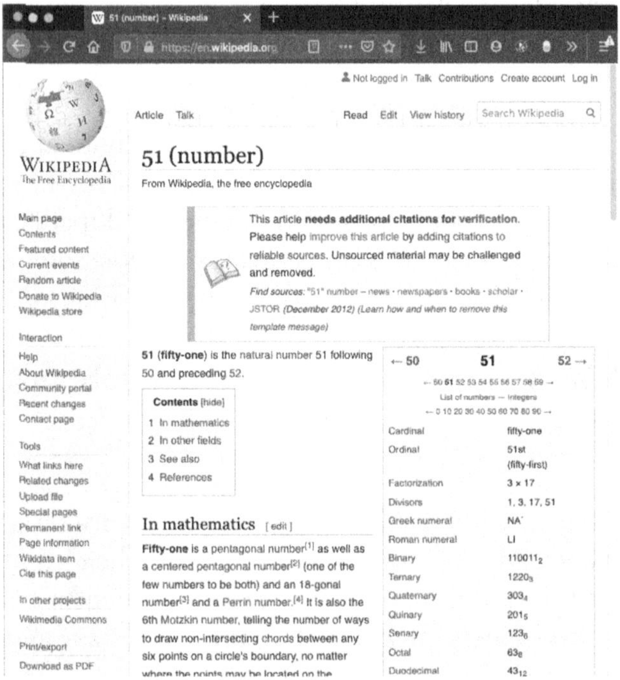


Figure 2.1: The Wikipedia page for the number 51 includes a helpful list of places the number appears in pop culture and is an excellent resource.

Halifax $\rightarrow$ 5160

I see Howard Brown (The star of a marketing campaign for Halifax between 2000 and 2004, see [Wikipedia, 2020a]) who is dressed as a Jedi as he enters the famous Mos Eisley Cantina. He activates his lightsaber as local Stormtroopers start firing at him, and deflects all the bolts into a dartboard, hitting the treble twenty every time.

It's useful to do something similar during everyday conversations. Here are some examples of using a link when talking:

- "It costs 7.47, like the plane."
- "He's won it 12, a dozen, times."
- "We'll be there at 24 past, like Jack Bauer would."[5]

When you add a 'checksum' like the above examples, it is a lot easier for listeners to remember the information you are giving them because in some sense you are giving the information twice.[6]

[5]You may find yourself modifying some of the times to make it easier to do this, that's fine.

[6]You will start to sound like a Bingo caller, but that's the point, Bingo callers sound like that so that fewer mistakes are made by the players.

## 2.3 Road deaths

If you asked me how many road deaths were due to excess speed in 2018.[7], I'd see this link:

Deaths $\rightarrow$ 'Immune'

The Major System is used to convert keywords to numbers. I'm going to use it on the keyword 'immune' to get my answer. I first remove the vowels from the keyword (actually I remove any letter that isn't in Table 2.1, but that's mostly the vowels). That gives me the following:

mmn

Each remaining letter matches a digit in the final number, a quick lookup in Table 2.1 gives:

332

That is the answer we are looking for: 332 people were killed in the UK in 2018 due to excess speed by drivers.[8]

There are several different tables that people use to do the conversion. I use the same one as [Brown, 2007] because that's where I first came across it. Table 2.1 shows the necessary lookup and some simple approaches for remembering it.

I've worked through this example very slowly; when you get used to the Major System, the conversions are very fast.

[7]This is the most recent data available at `https://www.gov.uk/government/statistical-data-sets/ras50-contributory-factors` at the time of writing.

[8]For your interest 'Driving too slow for conditions or slow vehicle (e.g. tractor)' killed exactly two people.

| Letter | Number | Explanation |
|---|---|---|
| s/z | 0 | 'z' for zero and 's' looks like 'z' |
| l | 1 | 'l' has one line |
| n | 2 | 'n' has two lines |
| m | 3 | 'm' has three lines |
| r | 4 | a capital R looks a bit like a backwards 4 |
| v | 5 | 'V' is the Roman numeral for 5 |
| b/p | 6 | b is sort of the same shape as 6, and p is its reflection |
| t | 7 | t sort of looks like a seven |
| ch/gh | 8 | All the good letters were taken |
| d/g | 9 | g is sort of the same shape as 9 and d is its reflection |

Table 2.1: The lookup table I (and Derren Brown) use to convert between letters and numbers.

Once you are happy with the process for moving from keywords to numbers, you'll find the Major System is a very useful way of recalling quite dense numbers. I find that the hard part is doing the reverse: coming up with a keyword that has the correct letters in it, so I wrote a web app to help me out. The script takes in a number and gives me a list of keywords that can all be converted to that number. There are similar converters available for other ways of doing the Major System. I use Major System often in this book; it frequently appears in linking images, but is also used extensively in Section 4.4 as part of the structure itself and as major part of the large accounting example in Section 5.4.

There are other, more recent, approaches that convert numbers into images. They include the Person-Action-Object System [Foer, 2012] and the similar Dominic System [O'Brien, 2016]. I prefer the Major System because I feel like the two newer systems have problems when they are dealing with sets of numbers with an uneven distribution, or indeed when the same number comes up repeatedly, like a year.[9]

The Major System is an excellent approach for converting something hard to remember (a string of numbers) into something easier to remember (a word). Numbers are something that many people need to remember so the Major System is quite popular. For your own work, you might find that you regularly need to memorise something that is intrinsically hard (dance movements, equations, drug doses) and you will develop your own system

[9]Both the other systems excel in memory competitions, which is their natural home.

for encoding them effectively.

## 2.4 Summary

This chapter talked about choosing keywords, creating an image link between two keywords, and discussed the Major System as a method for converting numbers into images.

The key points are:

1. When creating a link, use all five of your senses.

2. Strange, violent, or obscene images make better links than tame ones, but the most important thing is to make them *fun*.

3. It's effective to use external aids to come up with an image or a keyword.

4. Sometimes you don't want to use memory techniques, sometimes it's best to focus your energy on a different part of the process.

# Chapter 3

# Linked Lists

This chapter discusses the advantages, disadvantages, and effectiveness of the linked list memory structure. It's the first structure you are going to be formally introduced to because it's the simplest.

In other books the linked list is variously called the Chain Method [Singhal and Singhal, 2015], the Linking Method [O'Brien, 2016], the Link Method [Lorayne, 1958], the Linking Mnemonic [Higbee, 2001] or even the Linking System [Brown, 2007].

Compared to other structures in this book, the linked list is the fastest structure to build and the slowest to search. It's the simplest to understand but also the most fragile.

There are four examples in this chapter: the first shows the basic operation of a linked list and shows why it matters which direction a links goes in; the second shows that linked lists are a good choice for lists that keep growing and that you can add elements at both ends of a linked list; the third shows why you probably *shouldn't* add elements at both ends; and the fourth shows how you can use a separate list to compensate for some of a linked list's failings.

## 3.1 Tube stations

Consider that you want to learn all the stations on the Circle line of the London Underground. To keep the example short, we'll only look at the following stations:

- Liverpool Street
- Aldgate (old gate)
- Tower Hill
- Monument
- Cannon Street
- Mansion House
- Blackfriars
- Temple
- Embankment

I'm going to link the first station to the second, the second to the third, and so on, until our list of links looks like this:

Liverpool $\rightarrow$ Aldgate (old gate) $\rightarrow$ Tower Hill $\rightarrow$ Monument $\rightarrow$ Cannon $\rightarrow$ Mansion House $\rightarrow$ Blackfriars $\rightarrow$ Temple $\rightarrow$ Embankment

The first link is:

Liverpool $\rightarrow$ old gate

---

I see the goalmouth at Anfield, Liverpool's home stadium.[1] The goal is blocked completely by an old and tattered fence. There's a well worn gate in it, fully the height of the goal, blocking a triangular gap in the fence, meaning that the simple gate forms an 'A' shape. Shots on goal by opposition players are bouncing off it harmlessly.

The following links are:

Old gate $\rightarrow$ Tower

---

I see the ground around the goalmouth shaking. There's a loud rumble, and suddenly a massive tower (of the sort Rapunzel would be imprisoned in), thrusts its way though the ground and starts rising upwards with great speed, smashing the gate in the process.

[1] This works despite the fact I wouldn't be able to recognise Anfield, having never been there, nor for that matter having much of an interest in football - it's that the natural link Liverpool $\Longrightarrow$ 'quite into football' was lying around for me

I'm continuing the overall image here: I'm still at Anfield, but something is happening to the gate itself. I didn't have to keep the same frame of reference, but it's sometimes pleasant to do so as long as I'm still making distinct linking images. When doing this, be careful not to fall into the trap of 'telling yourself a story that involves these keywords in this order', which you might even have been taught in school.[2] In this particular example, the rest of the links do maintain a continuing frame of reference and you could indeed recite them as a story, but they are memorised as distinct images: I use all of the senses and concentrate on the links individually.

Tower Hill → Monument

The tower that previously erupted from the ground is still rising quickly, reaching an impossible height. As it rises, I start to see flashes of shapes embedded in the stone. When the tower's climb starts to slow, I can see that those shapes are the world's monuments, particularly the Eiffel Tower, embedded in the stone with features sticking out as though they had been melted into it.

[2] I happen to run a small fiction publishing project, and I can tell you that writing a *memorable* story is an extremely hard task at the best of times. While it *can* be done successfully ([Cooke, 2008] is a good example) it normally only works if you have someone else write the story for you.

| Monument $\rightarrow$ Cannon Street |
|---|
| I see the Tower is coming under fire! A battery of three enormous cannons are shooting up at it from the ground. Thin for its height, the tower is in danger of collapse as it takes more and more damage. |

Those four links follow the Circle line stations clockwise around from Liverpool Street. The key part of this is that each keyword links directly to the next:

Liverpool $\rightarrow$ Algate (old gate)
$\rightarrow$ Tower Hill $\rightarrow$ Monument $\rightarrow$ Cannon Street

It's time to define linked list properly.

**DEFINITION 4** *A* linked list *is a sequence of keywords in which each keyword is directly linked to the next in the sequence.*

This example started at Liverpool Street because I go there regularly. This turned out to be a mistake: I should have started with Hammersmith because then I wouldn't have had a later problem with the Hammersmith to Paddington section.[3]

To go over a linked list you start at the first element and follow the chain all the way to the end. It's a natural fit for times where you might have to work though a list such as transport systems or members of a governing

[3]The complete Circle Line is effectively a spiral rather than being a circle.

body, or step-by-step procedures such as instructions for tying a rescue knot or following a cake recipe.

A linked list is quick for you to build, naturally keeps the order of your keywords in place,[4] and also reflects the human tendency to, well, make lists of things.

There are three disadvantages of a linked list. First, if you have a linked list of 40 items, and your link between the 3rd and the 4th breaks down, then you've lost the rest of the list as well. For an example like tube stations this isn't so bad because you can work backwards from other stations and restructure your list, but it's terrible if you are five minutes into giving a lecture with 40 points you wanted to make. That's one of the things that makes a linked list quite fragile: it is only as strong as its weakest link, and the weakest link breaks sooner than you think it might. Indeed, if you have a list that is 40 elements long, and you get each link right 99% of the time, then you'll fail to get to the end nearly a third of the time.[5]

Secondly, it's hard to jump quickly to, say, the 10th, 17th, or 25th keywords in the list without starting at the top and counting. This doesn't matter for tube stations because it's rarely a useful question to ask of the list, but would matter for, say, lists of US presidents, or anything relating to times or places. An array (Chapter 4) would work better in those cases. In Section 3.5 I talk about 'skip lists', which can help with this issue.

Thirdly, it's hard to answer the question "Is Oak Wood

---

[4]All of the structures in the book 'sort of' do this, but none make it this easy.

[5]While this is true, you'll find that good links are actually more than 99% effective.

underground station on the Circle Line?", particularly if you have also used, as I have, a memory structure for the Piccadilly Line, the Victoria Line, and the Waterloo and City Line.[6] For that situation you want an entirely different structure. The normal way to search a linked list is to start at the top and check every element until the end, which can take a really long time for a big list. This worst-case scenario of checking every element can be reduced for certain lists: for example if you have stored a set of keywords in alphabetical order, then you can stop your search as soon as you reach a keyword that is alphabetically later, but that's still quite a lot of searching.

In the case of the Circle Line, I have never had to recall the 10th element of the list directly, so the linked list has been a reasonable option (I have come unstuck by the 'what line is Oak Wood underground station on?' question, but that's a reasonable trade-off for me).

I memorised this list in around 2012 when Blackfriars station was closed for refurbishment, so I now have to separately remember that Blackfriars is between my existing link from Manor House to Temple. Interestingly, one of the advantages of linked lists in Computer Science is that it's easier to add elements into the middle of a linked list. Unfortunately this ability doesn't translate well into human memory, and readers are advised not to change links after they have been built, except in very particular situations (See Section 3.4 for an example of when you might be able to change a list).

---

[6]Readers familiar with London have likely noted that one of these is much less impressive than the others.

### 3.1.1 Directionality

I'm building a clear direction into the links I'm making: later links destroy, emerge from, or challenge, earlier ones. This is because each keyword in my list will be linked to two others and I don't want one of the links to overwhelm the other.

Consider creating the image links for this structure(the words are randomly chosen for the example)

Teapot → Godzilla → Cheese

I'll need two links. I might try these:

| Teapot → Godzilla |
| --- |
| Godzilla is crushing thousands of tiny teapot warriors under his feet as he strides towards Tokyo. The teapot warriors look so forlorn with their little feet sticking out of their hard shells: they really thought their armour would protect them |

| Godzilla → Cheese |
| --- |
| Godzilla is using his atomic breath to irradiate all of the world's cheese as part of a financial scam. I can hear Shirley Bassey sing 'God-zilla' to the tune of 'Goldfinger' |

Those linking images are going to cause a problem when reviewing this later because they are both Godzilla happening *to* something, and the strong image is going to overwhelm the weak one (In this case, I'm far more likely to remember the image of the poor teapot warriors at the expense of the cheese one).[7]

However, if I instead have an image of cheese doing something to Godzilla rather than the other way around, then I will be much more likely to remember both the images. When I work though the chain I'm asking the question: 'Teapots, okay, what happens to the teapot? Oh, Godzilla, cool. Okay, what happens to Godzilla? Right, interesting, cheese'.

I can go through a linked list in the other direction by asking 'What did the keyword happen to?'. Being able to go both ways is often useful and I recommend that you practice going all the way through in both directions, both when you first commit a list to memory and when you are reviewing it.[8]

## 3.2 UFC champions

Consider that you want to remember the list of Ultimate Fighting Competition(UFC) Heavyweight Champions. There have been 21 since 1997:

1. Mark Coleman

[7] Chapter 5 covers other ways of solving this double link problem, but directionality is much better in general.

[8] What I describe in this chapter is what Computer Science calls a 'doubly linked' list, meaning that you can move both forward and backward in the list. Computer Science also has one-way lists which we can ignore because lists are automatically two-way in human memory.

2. Maurice Smith
3. Randy Couture
4. Bas Rutten
5. Kevin Randleman
6. Randy Couture
7. Josh Barnett
8. Ricco Rodriguez
9. Tim Sylvia
10. Frank Mir
11. Andrei Arlovski
12. Tim Sylvia
13. Randy Couture
14. Brock Lesnar
15. Cain Velasquez
16. Junior dos Santos
17. Cain Velasquez
18. Fabrício Werdum
19. Stipe Miocic
20. Daniel Cormier

21. Stipe Miocic

This example suits a linked list: it's rare that champions are referred to by their absolute number and the key information is 'who they beat to win the championship' and 'how they lost it'.[9] , This example also lets us demonstrate that it's easy to add new information when it arises, and that we can even add new information to both ends of the list.

Assume we already have already build a linked list that stores the champions from Coleman all the way to Velasquez's second reign. We now want to add Fabrcio Werdum so I create the following link:

$$\text{Velasquez} \rightarrow \text{Werdum}$$

Now when I iterate over the list, it ends with Werdum rather than Velasquez. I can keep adding links like this forever, regardless of how old the list is.

Next, consider that the UFC Heavyweight title replaced the UFC Superfight Championship, which had two holders. The first was Ken Shamrock, who was defeated by Dan Severn, who was in turn defeated by Mark Coleman above.

It turns out we can add elements easily to both ends of a linked list. So we can end up at:

$$\text{Shamrock} \rightarrow \text{Severn} \rightarrow \text{Coleman} \rightarrow \ldots \rightarrow \text{Werdum}$$

[9]The 'only' requirement to become the champion is to beat the current champion at an official event as opposed to something like snooker, where the world champion is crowned at a set world championship event.

The structure we end up with is still a classic linked list and can be traversed in both directions. You could confidently recite all the champions backwards from the present day champion or forwards from the first.

Many sports fans already have a version of this linked list in their head - asked to tell you the UFC heavyweight champions they would probably be able to visualise the moment when a new champion beat the old one.[10]

## 3.3 World heritage sites

Consider that you have built a linked list for world heritage sites in the UK.[11] It's a reasonable structure to use because the list grows somewhat regularly (the last entry was 2019). You have now been asked to recite the list.

How do you start?

Most of the answers boil down to 'pick one that you can already remember is in the list, and work backwards or forwards until you find one of the ends.[12] This is unsatisfactory for three reasons:

1. In this case you've been asked to recite them from the start; you will lose time hunting around for the start.

[10] Actually the title was stripped from five champions in a period of eight years, so it's not quite that clear, but the note stands.

[11] Using [Wikipedia, 2020b].

[12] Scandalously, Aristotle appears to promote this approach [Yates, 1992, p. 49], but he's talking about a different structure, which we cover in the next chapter.

2. You might genuinely not be able to remember any of the items on a list without an existing link to get there (this is more noticeable when you have many linked lists in your memory palace, but remains key); for example, if you have four lists of seven phone numbers each.

3. You'll never really know whether you have reached the end of a list when you reach Durham Castle and Cathedral or if you have forgotten the link to the next item.[13]

So it is important to separately remember the start of the list. Often this is implicit; for the other two examples in this chapter I have the natural links:

$$\text{Circle Line} \implies \text{first one is Liverpool Street}$$

$$\text{UFC Champions} \implies \text{first one is Ken Shamrock}$$

I have the natural link for the circle line because friends and I often meet at Liverpool Street and I have the natural link for the first UFC champion because I've read Ken Shamrock's book about the topic, so I don't have to worry about memorising the first element of the set.

If you have any doubt about being able to remember the first item of the list, then you must directly connect in that keyword to the broader structure. So while I might have:

$$\text{Circle Line} \implies \text{first one is Liverpool Street} \rightarrow \text{Algate} \rightarrow \ldots$$

[13]You have, Giant's Causeway was registered slightly before.

for one of my lists, I must definitely have:

$$\text{Heritage Sites} \rightarrow \text{Giants Causeway} \rightarrow \text{Durham Castle} \rightarrow \ldots$$

for another. This will be more obvious when we build full memory palaces later.

## 3.4 A broken list

Consider you have built a linked list

$$B \rightarrow A \rightarrow C \rightarrow D \rightarrow E \rightarrow F$$

and you are proud of it. Later you discover you have made a mistake, it should have been:

$$A \rightarrow B \rightarrow C \rightarrow D \rightarrow E \rightarrow F$$

Your options are:

1. Remember (either with an extra link or elsewhere ) your error and then untangle it every time you access.

2. Start from scratch.

3. Attempt to repair it.

The first option is less bad that it sounds (I do exactly that with the Circle Line example above). As you go through the process of building a memory palace you'll find almost everything that looks like simple structure has lots of extra details that need to be carried along (the UFC example didn't include the fact that the title was vacant five times during its history). With a simple error on a big memory structure, I'd be inclined to leave it rather than taking the risk of muddying the waters.

The second option, starting again from scratch, is worthwhile, but takes a long time. The rule here is: never re-use an image from the previous structure. If you used an image of John Major, the former British Prime Minister as a key image in the old structure, then you must absolutely use something else in the new one, otherwise you'll accidentally find yourself skipping between structures. After a few review cycles (obviously you only review the new structure), the old one will fade completely.

The third option is the hardest, but it can work. However, it can only work with Linked Lists and only under certain conditions.

You can replace the start portion of a linked list with a different linked list. By 'start portion', I mean a section of any length that starts at your normal starting point. This normal starting point must not be directly connected to another structure (so your starting point must be from a ' $\Longrightarrow$ ' rather than a ' $\rightarrow$ '). Note that this is when it *can* be done, rather than *should* be done.

Returning to the example, Figure 3.1 shows our replacement as a diagram. To make the repair I take the following steps:

1. Create the new linked list (in our example A $\rightarrow$ B) as an entirely new list, using none of the images of the old one.

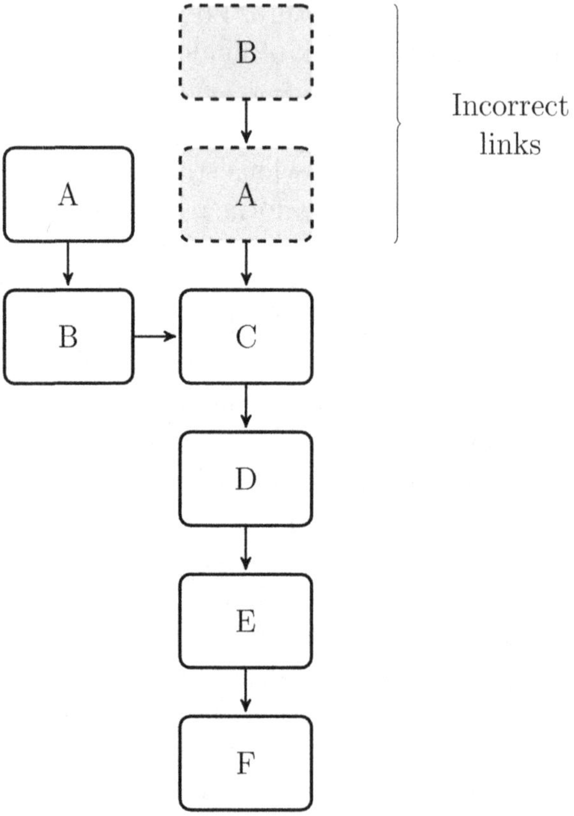


Figure 3.1: Altering a linked list by replacing the beginning section.

2. Create the link from your new list to the correct part of the old one (in our example B $\rightarrow$ C); spend a lot of time on this link and visualise it as completely as you can - it's the most risky link you'll make because it's replacing another one directly.

3. Review the new list several times, forward and backwards.

Obviously, the best course of action is to make sure that information is correct before it goes in. With all memory structures in this book, you should beware of trying to change them after they have been put into place - deleting a link is much much harder for humans than machines.

## 3.5 Skip lists

Consider that you have created a linked list of the 46 presidents of the United States and you are now having problems because presidents are often referred to by number, and it takes a lot of effort for you find the, say, 13th element on your list.

I have exactly such a list. With the aid of the excellent [Cleveland et al., 2017] I have a linked list for all 46 presidents of the United States.[14] In general terms, a linked list is the wrong structure for this information, but it's easier for me to use the work of [Cleveland et al., 2017] uses than create a different structure from scratch.

[14] To be unnecessarily honest, I have a list up to 40, because I can already remember the ones from my lifetime.

So we have a question: how can we speed up the search of a linked list?

One Computer Science solution is a *skip list*. Skip lists were created in 1989 by William Pugh [Pugh, 1990] and have complex and subtle ways of working. We are only going to implement the most basic level, but there are still significant issues to be aware of.

I'm going to create a separate second linked list that contains every tenth president as follows:

Washington (1st) → Tyler (10th) → Garfield (20th)

→ Coolidge (30th) → Reagan(40th)

Figure 3.2 shows part of the skip list and the linked list that it is anchored to.[15]

When I create the linked list, it is very important that I don't use the same set of keywords as the first one because I'd get them muddled up and ruin everything. The existing linked list uses 'washing' as a keyword for Washington, and so I'm going to use 'ink-ton', that is, a literal tonne of ink, for the skip list. The existing keyword for Tyler is 'Tie-lure' and I'm going to use 'tiler', as in 'person who lays tiles', for the skip list.

I'm also going to make sure that they are anchored separately. We'll learn about way of anchoring multiple links in the same class later, for now please assume that we have the link skip → 'ink-ton' available.

I use it as follows:

---

[15] I'm aware that Washington to Tyler is only nine links, but I wanted a starting point.

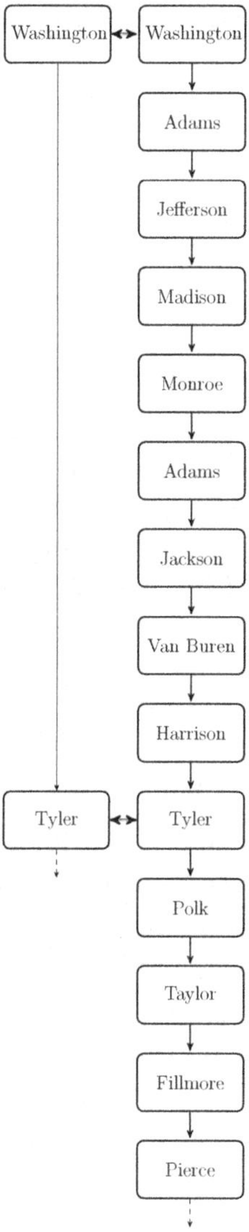


Figure 3.2: Part of a linked list of U.S presidents along with part of an associated skip list.

- I want to recall the 13th president.
- It's easier to get to the 13th president from the 10th than the first so I mentally turn to my skip list.
- The skip list records every tenth element of the main list so I follow the link 'ink-ton' → 'tiler' to find the closest one to 13.
- I follow the natural link 'tiler' ⟹ 'Tyler' to work out the 10th President and then use that to enter the original linked list at the 10th Position.
- I follow the links there through Polk (11th), Taylor (12th) to find Fillmore, who was indeed the 13th President.

Note that there are only natural links in my memory between the original list and the skip list. I keep them as separate as possible. The skip list lets me remember that a particular element has a particular number, and then I can step into the original list at that point, but there isn't any formal linking image.

I choose to make my links ten places apart, but you can use any number that fits for you. You can even simply remember a few 'landmarks' if you like.

A skip list is likely to be the first truly novel memory structure you've seen. It's only useful in certain circumstances: you have to be confident you can jump into the list at any point and keep going, and you also have to be happy to do a little more thinking to get quickly to the answer you are looking for. It's useful for lists you already know well but want to speed up your access for.

## 3.6 Summary

A linked list is best used when you want to be able to store a particular set of things in a particular order, but only if you are unlikely to need to recall, for example, the 53rd in the sequence. It's a structure that you add items to the end of (suiting, for example, ongoing histories, like the list of actors to play James Bond), and, to a slightly lesser extent, the beginning. Although you can't easily jump to a numbered item, you can quickly jump to a *known* item, so, if you have stored the stations on the Piccadilly Line of the London Underground as a linked list, then you can easily recall information like 'What are the stations adjacent to Hatton Cross?'. Linked lists are a fairly poor approach to recall things like US presidents (because US presidents are often referred to by their number), or FA cup finalists because they are invariably attached to a year.[16]

The key points of the chapter are:

1. Linked lists naturally suit ordered sets of keywords.
2. They are fragile but quick to create.
3. They can be traversed forwards or backwards.
4. New items can be added at either the start or end, and some lists can have additions at both ends, but only if you can reliably find a place to start on your own.

---

[16]These would be best managed by an array in both cases, see Chapter 4.

5. The links you create should have a clear directionality to them.

6. Some of the problems with a linked list can be reduced by using a second 'skip' list.

# Chapter 4

# Arrays

This is a large chapter. For the memorist, techniques like the Method of Loci, Memory walks, or the Peg System are very different techniques. However, for the computer scientist, they are all variations on one basic data-structure: the array. This chapter focuses on the fundamental properties of the array, shows how the memory techniques are variations on it, and gives some examples of how it can be used in yet more flexible ways.

Compared to other structures in the book, arrays are easy to look up information in ('What is the 14th item?') but quite slow to search ('Which items in this array are green?').[1] Arrays need some effort to build, but they are also long lasting and resilient.

There are eight examples in this chapter. I use the OPEC countries to show the basic use of an array, then

[1] In terms of searching, an array is actually slightly slower to search than a linked list, although both depend greatly on how the keywords are ordered.

I use a presentation to show that the Method of Loci is an example of an array, and then use my daughter's bag to show song lyrics can be used as rich set of source keywords for arrays. I use 'The Knowledge' to show how you can combine linked lists and arrays, and use Scrabble to make the point that acronyms are yet another form of array.[2] Finally, I use an array to make a 'good memories' room in our memory palace.

## 4.1 OPEC

Consider learning the names of the countries in Organization of the Petroleum Exporting Countries (OPEC) for an exam.

They are:

- Algeria
- Angola
- Congo
- Equatorial Guinea
- Gabon
- Iran

[2]Technical note for the computer scientists: the structures in this chapter look a lot like dictionaries or hash maps, but they are arrays: the nth item in the array is returned when the array is passed the nth item in another ordered set. You are used to that ordered set being the integers, but it really can be anything.

- Iraq
- Kuwait
- Libya
- Nigeria
- Saudi Arabia
- United Arab Emirates
- Venezuela

You could use the linked list approach you saw in Chapter 3. That would produce a structure that looked like:

Algeria → Angola → Congo → Equatorial Guinea → Gabon → Iran → Iraq → Kuwait → Libya → Nigeria → Saudi Arabia → United Arab Emirates → Venezuela

That would work, but you are worried that if you forget one of the keywords, you'll forget the whole rest of the sequence in the middle of the exam.

A safer structure would be an *array*. In an array we take a list of something we know well, and pair it up with the thing we are trying to learn.

For this example I'm using the list of the 13 major Batman movies of my lifetime[3] as my 'list I know well'. They are:

[3]This example is dedicated to a friend who used a similar system of films to store all the information he needed for his Anaesthetist exams.

- The four 90's ones:
  1. Batman
  2. Batman Returns
  3. Batman Forever
  4. Batman and Robin
- The Christopher Nolan trilogy:
  5. Batman Begins
  6. The Dark Knight
  7. The Dark Knight Rises
- The DC expanded universe set:
  8. Batman versus Superman
  9. Suicide Squad
  10. Justice League
- The Lego set:
  11. The Lego Movie
  12. Lego Batman
  13. The Lego Movie 2: The Second Part

The important thing about the set of films is that I can remember it perfectly with little effort.

Section 2.1 said concrete nouns make the best keywords: so instead of linking from the film itself I used the main antagonist of each film as the source keywords.[4] It's really useful to be consistent in these circumstances, I never want to be thinking 'which character did I use as the linking point?'.

I'm now going to create 13 links between the elements of the set I know, and the elements of the set I'm memorising. In the case of Angola and Equatorial Guinea, I link from the film to a keyword that has its own natural link to the desired country, and I show that using the $\Longrightarrow$ symbol. The structure is:

1. Joker (Batman) $\rightarrow$ Algeria
2. Penguin (Batman Returns) $\rightarrow$ Ang Lee $\Longrightarrow$ Angola
3. Riddler (Batman Forever) $\rightarrow$ Congo
4. Mr Freeze (Batman and Robin) $\rightarrow$ A Guinea Pig $\Longrightarrow$ Equatorial Guinea
5. Scarecrow (Batman Begins) $\rightarrow$ Gabon
6. Other Joker (The Dark Knight) $\rightarrow$ Iran
7. Bane (The Dark Knight Rises) $\rightarrow$ Apple's Wine Storage System (Iraq)
8. Superman (Batman V Superman) $\rightarrow$ Kuwait
9. Enchantress (Suicide Squad) $\rightarrow$ Libya

[4]Purists will have issues with some of my choices, but these are the characters I naturally think of as the antagonist and it's my memory...

10. Steppenwolf (Justice League) → Nigeria
11. Lord Business (Lego Movie) → Saudi Arabia
12. Lego Joker (Lego Batman) → United Arab Emirates
13. Rex Dangervest (Lego Movie 2) → Venezuela

I now make the following links:

Jack Nicholson's Joker → Algeria

---

I see Nicholson's Joker using his signature poisoned makeup on the giant and quite sleepy figure of Al Bundy from the show Married with Children (Algeria is the largest country in Africa so 'Giant Al' is a natural short-cut)

Penguin → Ang Lee

---

I see Danny Deveto's Penguin running up walls in the Wushu style of Crouching Tiger Hidden Dragon

Riddler → Congo

---

Jim Carey's Riddler has a magic puzzle box for me! Except that when I solve the puzzle, I'm swept away by the massive force of the entire Congo River that erupts out of the box.

Mr Freeze → A Guinea Pig

---

I see a frozen Guinea pig. Like completely frozen. It shatters. It's completely gross.

Scarecrow → Gabon

---

I see the villain Scarecrow jumping out to terrify a passer by, but is thwarted by a mighty defensive spell in the form of a Phoenix - the Patronus of Albus Dumbledore himself (played by Michael Gambon)

Heath Ledger's Joker → Iran

---

I see Heath Ledger's Joker doing his famous speech, only it's about the exercise app Strava "Want to know how I got all this Kudos?", which gives me 'I Ran'

Bane → Apple's Wine Storage System

---

I see Bane in a Wine cellar, monologuing "Ah Bruce, you only adopted Apple products, I was born to them..." while holding a very fancy Wine Storage System: the I-rack

Superman → Kuwait

I see Superman brutally, really nastily, beating Jame Bond's Q to a pulp with a dumbbell in the weights room of a gym. There's blood all over the 'S' on his chest, it's really horrible

Enchantress → Libya

This is something of an individual one - when I try and visualise the Enchantress from Suicide Squad I actually see a character called 'Unknown' from a particular fighting game. Co-incidentally when I try and think about Muammar Gaddafi, the former ruler of Libya, I always end up thinking of M.Bison, a character from another fighting game, thus my image for this link is M.Bison and Unknown fighting using their trademark moves.

Steppenwolf → Nigeria

The Monstrous Steppenwolf, is fighting an agent from The Matrix, who is wearing a giant ornate crown ('Reign AI' is an anagram of 'Nigeria')

Lord Business → Saudi Arabia

The Lego Lord Business is busily supergluing (Kraggling!) a Lego crown on his head for the Kingdom of Saudi Arabia.[5]

Lego Joker → United Arab Emirates

I see life scale Lego model, in the joker's colours, of the Burj Khalifa, the tallest building in both the UAE and the world.

Rex Dangervest → Venezuela

Rex Dangervest is Playing Hardcore-Man-Poker with a Lego Hugo Chavez (former president of Venezuela), wearing his army uniform with red beret, before the end of the game Chavez has swept to power, taking over Rex's ship.

That's the largest set of links we have built so far in this book. The links let me move from one set of items I can already recall to another set that I am trying to memorise. I can now recite the 13 countries of OPEC without much effort. Also, if I forget one link, then I

[5]You might think that this is a risky link because, e.g. the UAE is also a monarchy, but it works for me (it helps that the UAE doesn't refer to its royals as 'king').

only forget one element of the target set.

**DEFINITION 5** *An* array *is a mapping of elements between two lists, the source and the target, in which:*

- *Every keyword in the target list is linked to by at least one keyword in the source.*

- *The source list is ordered.*

This example has some issues:

- Consistently using the film antagonist got me into trouble because I ended up with 'The Joker' as three of the keywords. Fortunately, the three different versions of the Joker are different enough that I didn't have a major problem, but it certainly could have been one.

- I didn't take this example quite seriously enough when storing them (I had trouble with Congo and Gabon particularly). It was a useful reminder that it's important to really take the time to craft the linking image.

- The set of films is badly chosen because the order isn't ideal: the DC expanded universe films are all released after the Lego Movie but before its sequel, and so there isn't a natural order of recall.

It still works very well, but I could have designed it much better.

## 4.2 Your presentation

Consider that you have a presentation to give. You have a particular set of points to make and you want to make sure you hit them all. The keywords to hit are:

- Help
- Understood
- Title
- Enthusiastic
- Glow
- Absurd
- Far
- Ray

As before, I could use a linked list for this one, but we aren't going to for safety reasons: if a link fails then we want to smoothly move onto the next one. I'm going to use an array, so we need an ordered set of source keywords to link to.

I am going find the source keywords in the presentation room itself so I physically go to the room in advance. I need eight source keywords so I work clockwise around the room and pick the most obvious and eye-catching object in the middle of each wall and in each corner. In this example those are going to be: the presentation screen, the lectern, the painting of the polar bears, the fire exit, the table with hot drinks and biscuits on it, the light switches and the main entrance. So I am going to make the following links:

1. The screen $\rightarrow$ help
2. The lectern $\rightarrow$ understood
3. The painting of polar bears $\rightarrow$ title
4. The fire exit $\rightarrow$ enthusiastic
5. The table with hot drinks $\rightarrow$ glow
6. The light switches $\rightarrow$ absurd
7. The main entrance $\rightarrow$ far
8. The potted plant $\rightarrow$ ray

Once the links are put in, is easy to glance clockwise around the room, pick out the eight objects that you'd chosen, and recall the target keywords.

At the risk of repeating myself, arrays are a way of relating the thing you want to memorise to something you already know *or* something you can quickly work out.

Memorists would call this example the *Method of Loci*, and it's our first example that looks and feels like a 'true' memory palace.

The Method of Loci so dominates memory palaces in popular culture that almost all the comments when I sent out this book's cover design for feedback were some form of 'It should show what a memory palace should look like, maybe have a house with lots of labels on it'.

If I was strictly keeping to the conventions of this book I would refer to any use of the Method of Loci as 'an array that is indexed by physical locations', but that would be childish of me. To reflect the dominance of the Method of Loci in the popular imagination, I'll refer to it as such in this book,[6] but you should always remember that there is nothing special about it. The term 'Method of Loci' is a shorthand for 'using physical locations as a source of keywords for an array'. Sections 4.3 and 4.7 contain some other rich examples of sources of keywords.[7]

It's important that the objects you choose in the room are regular and obvious. If I had chosen eight objects scattered around the room, then it is likely I would have forgotten them quickly. Instead I had a very clear rule: the most obvious item in the middle of each wall and in each corner.

Different rooms can have different layouts: I have 16 points (top and bottom of each corner, and top and bottom of the centre of each wall) in an old bathroom that help me remember Kipling's poem If, and 13 (five down each wall and three at the end) in my university's old chapel to help me remember my most treasured memories, but each room must have some clear structure for picking out your source objects.[8]

---

[6]It occasionally gets called 'roman room' or 'a memory walk' in popular texts.

[7]Historically, of course, there *is* something special about the Method of Loci, it was the prime method taught, discussed, and used. [Yates, 1992].

[8]The ancient approach is to put some special symbol or image after every fifth keyword, but I've never been able to get that to work reliably.

You don't need to be physically in the same room when you recall the objects:[9] it's often easier to work through the objects when you aren't in the room. The room doesn't even have to be real: computer game worlds often have nice setups.[10]

Many people find that using rooms to remember sets of information is natural, particularly because there is a ready supply of new rooms to map. It may well be that using rooms or physical locations as arrays forms the vast majority of your memory palace.

If you are using a room or building to memorise a set of information, it's often worth using older buildings, because they generally have more features of interest that you can hang a hook on.

I do sometimes use this process for particularly long talks that are very data heavy and where the language matters less: I have a lecture I give on the 52 Java keywords, that I memorised a decade ago using rooms in my office building at the time.[11] I can still give it easily assuming that a) Java comes back into fashion and b) anyone ever asks.

---

[9]Particularly if someone removes the potted plant.

[10]Indeed, virtual worlds have been shown to be equally effective [Legge et al., 2012], although I personally have never found them successful.

[11]It's worth noting that for the Java example, I used one image per room, and the source of links was actually the order of rooms as I walked down the corridor.

## 4.3 My daughter's bag

A little over 20 years ago a friend lamented to me that if his memory for exam content was the equal of his memory for song lyrics, then we would have a far easier time at college. I happily dedicate this section to him.

I need to make sure that the following items go with my daughter to the childminder:

- Nappy bag
- Snack
- Drink
- Spare clothes
- Sunhat
- Sunscreen
- Tissues

If I wanted to memorise these[12] in an array, then I'd want a set of seven source keywords to connect my links with.

I'm going to use one of my daughter's nursery rhymes.[13] I've chosen this one:

[12] I don't. This is a great example of something you shouldn't memorise because it changes depending on season, day, and age of child; I actually have this written on a bit of paper in a clear pocket in the front of her bag.

[13] In case you are wondering, it costs a fortune to use song lyrics in published books, which is why this is a short example using a public domain nursery rhyme rather than a detailed discussion of 20th Century music.

> This old man, he played one, He played knick-knack on my thumb, With a knick-knack paddywhack, Give a dog a bone, This old man came rolling home.

If I look at only the nouns in the lyrics (and ignore any doubles) I have the following seven terms:

- Old Man
- One
- Knick-knack
- Paddywhack
- Dog
- Bone
- Home

This is a nice set of keywords that I can link with my targets.[14] The links themselves are left as an exercise. For the right person, the back catalog of their favourite musical artist is an enormous repository of source keywords.

[14]There has been some comment on if 'one' is a noun or an adjective; I've used it as a noun here because it's a short example but normally I'd skip numbers because they are harder to add links to.

## 4.4 Oscar winners

Consider the idea of building a structure to hold the winners of the Best Picture Oscar between 2000 and 2019 to your list. You are going to use the set of years as the array, for the obvious reason that there is one Oscar for each year. The twenty most recent look like this:

- 2019 → Parasite
- 2018 → Green Book
- 2017 → The Shape of Water
- 2016 → Moonlight
- 2015 → Spotlight
- 2014 → Birdman
- 2013 → 12 Years a Slave
- 2012 → Argo
- 2011 → The Artist
- 2010 → The King's Speech
- 2009 → The Hurt Locker
- 2008 → Slumdog Millionaire
- 2007 → No Country for Old Men
- 2006 → The Departed

- 2005 → Crash
- 2004 → Million Dollar Baby
- 2003 → The Lord of the Rings: The Return of the King
- 2002 → Chicago
- 2001 → A Beautiful Mind
- 2000 → Gladiator

Years are exceptionally difficult to visualise and they are even harder to do so in a way that is reliable for your memory palace.

I find some years easy to find images for: I moved to Scotland in 2010, I was in London for the 2012 Olympics and I volunteered during the 2015 general election in the UK so I can easily find images that match those years. I could totally use those as source images for my links except that I could only use them like that once. If I used an image of the 2012 Olympics to remember Oscar winners, then I wouldn't be able to use it as part of a link when I later add other annual events to my palace like sports competitions, festival line ups or yearly GDP figures.

I've decided to use intermediate keywords. I want to be able to easily translate the year to a physical object and then link that new keyword to my target keyword. It would mean a two-step process, but it would be much more effective to use a series of simple steps than one hard one.

A good idea would be to use the Major System from Section 2.3 to convert the years into keywords, particularly as I only need the last two digits. However, if I ever wanted to memorise other information that involved the year, then I'd need to find another method. To avoid this, I'll use the Major System with one small modification: all words must start with the letter 'f' for film. That way if I want to use the years again later for, say, economic indicators, I can use the same method but start every hook with the letter 'e'.

Here's what my new structure looks like. It uses natural links to go from the year to a useful keyword, which can be more easily linked to the film title.

- 2019 $\Longrightarrow$ f19 $\Longrightarrow$ flg $\Longrightarrow$ flag $\rightarrow$ Parasite
- 2018 $\Longrightarrow$ f18 $\Longrightarrow$ flsh $\Longrightarrow$ flash $\rightarrow$ Green Book
- 2017 $\Longrightarrow$ f17 $\Longrightarrow$ flt $\Longrightarrow$ filet $\rightarrow$ The Shape of Water
- 2016 $\Longrightarrow$ f16 $\Longrightarrow$ flp $\Longrightarrow$ flap $\rightarrow$ Moonlight
- 2015 $\Longrightarrow$ f15 $\Longrightarrow$ flf $\Longrightarrow$ facelift $\rightarrow$ Spotlight
- 2014 $\Longrightarrow$ f13 $\Longrightarrow$ flr $\Longrightarrow$ flare $\rightarrow$ Birdman
- 2013 $\Longrightarrow$ f13 $\Longrightarrow$ flm $\Longrightarrow$ film $\rightarrow$ 12 Years a Slave
- 2012 $\Longrightarrow$ f12 $\Longrightarrow$ fln $\Longrightarrow$ flan $\rightarrow$ Argo
- 2011 $\Longrightarrow$ f11 $\Longrightarrow$ fll $\Longrightarrow$ flail $\rightarrow$ The Artist
- 2010 $\Longrightarrow$ f10 $\Longrightarrow$ fls $\Longrightarrow$ files $\rightarrow$ The King's Speech

- 2009 $\Longrightarrow$ f09 $\Longrightarrow$ fzg $\Longrightarrow$ Fizgig $\rightarrow$ The Hurt Locker
- 2008 $\Longrightarrow$ f08 $\Longrightarrow$ fsch $\Longrightarrow$ "F*** school" $\rightarrow$ Slumdog Millionaire
- 2007 $\Longrightarrow$ f07 $\Longrightarrow$ fst $\Longrightarrow$ fist $\rightarrow$ No Country for Old Men
- 2006 $\Longrightarrow$ f06 $\Longrightarrow$ fsb $\Longrightarrow$ fuseboard $\rightarrow$ The Departed
- 2005 $\Longrightarrow$ f05 $\Longrightarrow$ F5 $\Longrightarrow$ F5 (wrestling move) $\rightarrow$ Crash
- 2004 $\Longrightarrow$ f04 $\Longrightarrow$ fcr $\Longrightarrow$ Facer (lathe) $\rightarrow$ Million Dollar Baby
- 2003 $\Longrightarrow$ f03 $\Longrightarrow$ fsm $\Longrightarrow$ Flying Spaghetti Monster $\rightarrow$ The Lord of the Rings: The Return of the King
- 2002 $\Longrightarrow$ f02 $\Longrightarrow$ fsn $\Longrightarrow$ fusion $\rightarrow$ Chicago
- 2001 $\Longrightarrow$ f01 $\Longrightarrow$ fsl $\Longrightarrow$ fusilli (pasta) $\rightarrow$ A Beautiful Mind
- 2000 $\Longrightarrow$ f00 $\Longrightarrow$ fss $\Longrightarrow$ fuses $\rightarrow$ Gladiator

The final set of keywords is a little bit adjusted from the method described above: Fizgig (a character from the TV series *The Dark Crystal*) isn't spelt that way, and I inserted other entries for 2003, 2005, and 2008 because the Major System didn't have good options for those (importantly, my changed entries keep the 'f' at the start).

I'm happy with those being minor adjustments and I'm confident they won't damage the overall effectiveness of the process. This structure gives me two natural links to go from any year to an image that represents that year *in the context of films.* I try and make it a rule to review the table thoroughly before I add the actually important information, although it's often possible to do that quickly with paper and pen.

Now I've got a way to move from years to intermediate keywords, the actual image links are relatively straightforward. The first few look like this:

| Flag → Parasite |
| --- |
| I see a flag - it's the South Korean Flag! It's flying, but being sadly ravaged by all manner of bugs - some sort of parasite is eating it from the inside! |

| Flash → Green Book |
| --- |
| I see Flash Gordon, with the full Queen soundtrack from the 1980 film, crash-landing into the concert hall from the Green Book, there's rubble everywhere. |

| Filet → The Shape of Water |
| --- |
| I see a filet of fish, but it's a bit more raw than I would expect; it turns out to have been carved out of the living flesh of the amphibious humanoid creature from The Shape of Water. |

This process of having a set of intermediate keywords based on numbers is what memorists call the 'Peg System'.[15]

This example didn't introduce any new information about arrays as such, but it did show how to construct one using years as a key. It's included because 'year' is a really common way of indexing an array, and because the intermediate keyword technique I used here is extremely useful on its own: I demonstrate another variant in Section 4.6.

## 4.5 Keyboard shortcuts

Consider that you want to memorise the set of keyboard shortcuts to use the autocomplete function in the text editor Vim.[16]

[15]Remarkably, given the variety of names we saw in Chapter 3 and in Section 4.2, everybody calls it the Peg System without any variation.

[16]Vim is the editor I'm using to write this book, it's famously complex and difficult (but powerful) to use and I've never actually tried to use this function before.

| | |
|---|---|
| Whole lines | i_CTRL-X,CTRL-L |
| keywords in the current file | i_CTRL-X,CTRL-N |
| keywords in 'dictionary' | i_CTRL-X,CTRL-K |
| keywords in 'thesaurus', | i_CTRL-X,CTRL-T |
| keywords in current and included files | i_CTRL-X,CTRL-I |
| tags | i_CTRL-X,CTRL-] |
| file names | i_CTRL-X,CTRL-F |
| definitions or macros | i_CTRL-X,CTRL-D |
| Vim command-line | i_CTRL-X,CTRL-V |
| User defined completion | i_CTRL-X,CTRL-U |
| omni completion | i_CTRL-X,CTRL-O |
| Spelling suggestions | i_CTRL-X,s |
| keywords in 'complete' | i_CTRL-N and CTRL-P |

Table 4.1: The 14 Vim shortcuts for autocompletion.

Vim has 14 different shortcuts for autocompletion,[17] shown in the Table 4.1.

For your interest 'CTRL-X' means 'Press the Control key and x at the same time' and the prefix 'i_' means 'you can only do this in the insert mode'.

The first step is to boil the information down to the minimum I have to remember. The common factors I need to remember are that all except two of the shortcuts start with CTRL-X and that all except one need the Control key.[18]

I can split the shortcuts into three groups: eight that have naturally obvious memory shortcut keys, four that

[17]It actually has more (I wasn't kidding about how complex it is), but these are the ones I want to commit to memory.

[18]I'm personally going to ignore the 'except one' because I naturally remember that pretty well and I don't believe I'll need help with it.

don't, and the two that don't use 'CTRL-X'.

- Natural Mnemonics
  - Whole (L)ines
  - (T)hesaurus words
  - (D)efinitions or macros
  - (F)ilenames
  - (U)ser defined completion
  - (O)mni completion
  - (V)im command-line
  - (S)pelling suggestions
- Harder links
  - keywords in the current file (N)
  - keywords in current and included files (I)
  - Dictionary words (K)
  - tags (])
- the two that don't use 'CTRL-X'.
  - keywords in 'complete' (N and P)

In the circumstances I might be looking at three fairly short linked lists, or one longer one with markers on it. However, after a short period of thinking, I find a natural array for the information.

I'm going to use the characters from the 2000 film 'X-Men' (which gives me the 'CTRL-X' I need for free). The film's mutant characters can be divided into three groups, firstly the eight heroic 'official' X-Men:

- Storm
- Cyclops
- Iceman
- Pyro
- Jubilee
- Professor X
- Jean Gray
- Shadowcat

There are also four antagonists:

- Magneto
- Toad
- Mystique
- Sabretooth

Moreover, there are also two heroic characters that aren't (at the start) X-Men:

- Wolverine
- Rogue

In a remarkably pleasing way, this naturally reflects the subcategories I wanted.

For brevity, I'll link only a couple of examples here. The first set are simple because the shortcut is built into the keyword:

| Jean Gray → (L)ines |
| --- |
| Jean Gray is on stage in a big theatre, but she stutters and stumbles because she can't remember her lines so she uses her telepathic powers to read them directly out of the mind of the prompter. Really useful. |

The second set aren't much harder, although they do end up forming extremely short linked lists.

| Magneto → Words in current file |
| --- |
| Magneto wants to grab a perfectly ordinary file from a filing cabinet, but every time he tries, he magnetically attracts another large steel wood file that painfully attaches to him until he is almost trapped under the weight |

| Words in current file → The Letter N |
| --- |
| The steel file has become the tusk of a narwhal, which it is using to cunningly attack the wooden hulls of whaling ships. |

Without going too much into the details, here is the full set of links I made

- Cyclops → (D)efinitions
- Iceman → (F)ilenames
- Jean Gray → (L)ine
- Jubilee → (O)mni completion
- Professor X → (S)pelling suggestions
- Pyro → (T)hesaurus
- Shadowcat → (U)ser completion
- Storm → (V)im command line
- Magneto → Current → N
- Mystique → Dictionary Words → K
- Sabretooth → Included files → I
- Toad → Tags → ]
- Rogue → Backward completion → P
- Wolverine → forward completion → N

This has been a fairly long example, and it's designed to illustrate some important notes:

- Choosing the right set of hooks for your array is important, and it's worth taking some care over.

- Some sets of hooks naturally have subcategories and these can be exploited.
- It's important to work out exactly what it is that you are trying to remember before choosing a structure.
- Inbuilt structure helps everywhere - the mutants in each category appear alphabetically, as do the shortcuts - giving me a tiny bit more information if I'm struggling to complete the set.

When I built this example I did some things wrong. The Jean Gray example was originally about Storm, but I moved the pairings around because I wanted to make both sides alphabetical. When I came to update the image, I found that I didn't have to change anything about the description I had to make it about another character, which means that it was a very poor description indeed.[19] The lesson here is: don't be lazy.

## 4.6 The Knowledge

Consider that you want to memorise the necessary information to pass the London Taxi Driver exam. This is known as 'The Knowledge' and is famously hard. You can be tested on 360 set routes of around 20 streets each.[20]

An example set of routes are:

[19]It's still relatively poor, because the same image can apply to at least one other character, possibly more.

[20]There's more to it; I've made it simpler for the purpose of the example.

1. Islington Police Station to British Museum
2. Manor House Station, N4 to Gibson Square, N1
3. Thornhill Square, N1 to Queen Square, WC1
4. Chancery Lane Station, WC1 to Rolls Road, SE1
5. Pages Walk, SE1 to St. Martins Theatre, WC2
6. Australian High Commission, WC2 to Paddington Station, W2

The streets for the first route, Islington Police Station to British Museum, are:

1. Left onto Tolpuddle Street
2. Left onto Penton Street
3. Forward onto Claremont Square
4. Forward onto Amwell Street
5. Right onto Margery Street
6. Forward onto Calthorpe Street
7. Forward onto Guilford Street
8. Left then right around Russell Square
9. Left onto Montague Street
10. Right onto Great Russell Street
11. Set down on right

Where possible, have a structure that matches the information's own structure. We do this by connecting two basic structures together. I'm going to have a large array for the 360 routes, and each one of those arrays will point to a linked list that stores the sequence of roads.

The first step is always to work out exactly what I'm memorising. Each route in The Knowledge starts at a different place[21] so I only need to keep the starting point in the array - the end of the route will be at the end of the linked list. I can also take out the left and right turns because I believe that anyone taking The Knowledge can probably deduce that from context either while driving or during the exam. Lastly, I've taken out words like 'street' or 'road' from the routes for the same reason.

My next step is to plan the main array. It needs to be large enough to store 360 keywords, and each of those keywords will be a place, so I need a set of 360 source keywords that are easy to link to places.

The Method of Loci would be a bad idea for two reasons:

1. 360 keyword hooks is quite a lot to find in a location.

2. each of the keyword hooks in a Method of Loci array is a physical location, and it can be hard to link two sets of physical locations together (try it yourself by linking the set above with the sources in Section 4.2).

Finding 360 source keywords that I know well enough to use as the basis of an array would be near-impossible,

[21] I believe this is true, but only because I had a quick look just now.

so I'm going to generate some intermediate keywords like I did in Section 4.4. I'm going to use pairs of letters. I start with 'AA', 'AB', and 'AC', and keep going until I run out of routes.[22] For each letter pair I'm going to use the first famous person I think of with those initials as the keyword. My first few links will be:

1. AA $\Longrightarrow$ Alexander Armstrong $\rightarrow$ Islington Police Station
2. AB $\Longrightarrow$ Angela Bassett $\rightarrow$ Manor House Station
3. A(O)C $\Longrightarrow$ Alexandria Ocasio-Cortez $\rightarrow$ Thornhill Square
4. AD $\Longrightarrow$ Adam Driver $\rightarrow$ Chancery Lane Station
5. AE $\Longrightarrow$ Albert Einstein $\rightarrow$ Pages Walk
6. AF $\Longrightarrow$ Anne Frank $\rightarrow$ Australian High Commission

This gives me an array that is big enough and provides a rich set of sources that will be straightforward to link to the locations.

These letter pairs are another example of the intermediate keywords introduced in Section 4.4 except this time we're starting from letters rather than years.

The last step is to build a linked list for each route. The diagram below shows the linked list for the first route.

[22] I think I run out at 'MV'.

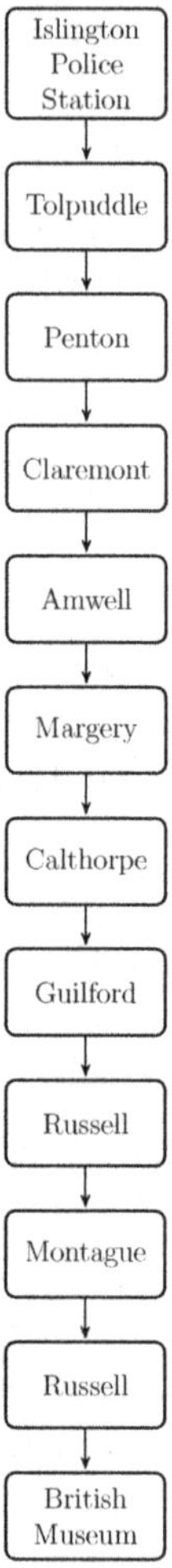


This is a nice solution:

- I have an easy way of going through the routes, and I've picked a set of intermediate keywords that are easy to link to the routes.

- I've used the advantages of an array where I wanted them: one broken link will have a very limited effect overall

- I've used the advantages of a linked list in a place where its disadvantages matter less: if I reach Guilford Street, I'm going to see Russell Square in time to be reminded even if the link is failing

For what it's worth, I don't think The Knowledge should be learned this way; much better to handle it the old fashioned way by cycling around London.

The concept of combining our basic structures to match the structure of the information doesn't appear in traditional memory books, but it is central to building an effective memory palace.

## 4.7 Scrabble

Consider you have started playing scrabble and would like to be better at it. It's useful for Scrabble players to know the 107 two letter words[23] that can be played. These include obvious ones like 'in', and less obvious ones like 'jo'.[24]

I would normally now work through the best way of structuring a list of 107 words in memory, but it's already been done well by the blogger Tom Rees who gives a detailed breakdown on his website [Rees, 2012]. He converts

[23] Assuming they are playing it in English.

[24] An old word for sweetheart.

the problem from 'learn over a hundred words' to 'learn ten phrases'.

Each phrase is a 'first letter mnemonic':[25] if Tom wants to know the valid words that end in 'u' he follows a link to the phrase 'onyx gem' - every consonant in that phrase can be followed by a 'u' to form a valid scrabble word.[26] He has another phrase for the letters that can go after 'u' to make a valid word, and a similar pair for each of the other vowels.

The scrabble example is in this chapter because first letter mnemonics are a type of memory array. Remember that the array definition is:

**DEFINITION 6** *An* array *is a mapping of elements between two lists, the source and the target, in which:*

- *Every keyword in the target list is linked to by at least one keyword in the source.*
- *The source list is ordered.*

In this case, the source list is 'the consonants in the phrase "Onyx Gem" and the target list is 'letters that can come before 'u' to make valid two-letter scrabble words'. Interestingly, in this example the links themselves are redundant - there is no need to create a strong image to help you do 'x' → 'x'.

[25]The term comes from [Higbee, 2001] but doesn't appear much in other books, although it enjoys a certain number of search results in the education literature. I suspect this is because this approach is unsuitable for competition or showing off.

[26]Tom's system was written up in 2012 and the official scrabble lists have changed since then, but his code is available for anyone that wants to generate new phrases.

Simple first letter mnemonics are common. At Primary school I learned the order of the planets in the solar system by the mnemonic 'My Very Easy Method Just Speeds Up Naming Planets' (Mercury, Venus, Earth, Mars, Jupiter, Saturn, Uranus, Neptune, and Pluto).[27]

The planetary mnemonic links the source list 'The first letter of each word in this phrase' to the list 'planets in the solar system' using the link 'this planet begins with this letter'.

Of course, that is the main problem: 'begins with this letter' is a weak link. It's great for planets, because you probably know them but need a hint, but it falls down rapidly whenever structures get big. A second problem is that you can't add things to them later - they are stuck as they are created, and a third is that you can have problems when you need to remember the order of two items that start with the same letter.

First letter mnemonics are particularly good when you know the material, but want to quickly go through to make sure that nothing has been missed: as such they are used a lot in medicine [Yousaf, 2006] and aviation.

In general, I think first letter mnemonics are extremely powerful and remarkably quick to create for short sets of information. They are included here to show how flexible the definition of an array is, and to illustrate an undervalued technique.

---

[27]At the time Pluto was a planet. There is an entire Wikipedia Page devoted to planetary mnemonics including post-Pluto ones and dwarf planets at `https://en.wikipedia.org/wiki/Planetary_mnemonic`.

## 4.8 Keyboard shortcuts again

Consider that you want to memorise the set of shortcuts for Vim's autocomplete function. This is the same situation as Section 4.5, but we are going to handle it differently.

This time I'm going to use a first letter mnemonic and create the following link:

$$\text{Vim shortcuts} \rightarrow 14 \rightarrow \text{Flout Pink DSV}$$

The phrase 'Flout pink DSV' is a first letter mnemonic for giving me the same set of letter shortcuts as Section 4.5 did. It's not perfect: it doesn't include the ']' shortcut, it doesn't actually give information on what the letters *do*, and there isn't a reminder that there are two different 'n' shortcuts [28] but it's the one I actually ended up putting in my memory palace.

I included this example as a cautionary tale; Section 4.5 showed an elegant method that included a nice way of partitioning the shortcuts and I loved how it came together; but it also required a lot of work to learn the links and create the images I needed. On top of this, it was massive overkill for the information I was trying to store, particularly since I now regularly use many of those shortcuts in my natural workflow. Because I regularly use the shortcuts, it's a lot easier for me to recall them naturally and they need less of a structure supporting them.[29] In short, don't spend more time than you need to on examples.

[28] This is why the 14 is in this series of links.

[29] This, of course, is surely the point of remembering them.

## 4.9 Good memories

Consider that you never want to forget the time you jumped off a bridge in rural New England to impress a girl.[30] In fact, you have written out a list of 15 wonderful experiences that you want to keep close to you. This is an extremely, if not *exactly* useful, fulfilling thing to do and I highly recommend it. You have a whole set of structures available to you, any of the ones in previous chapters would work. I would suggest a simple Method of Loci because:

- There is something viscerally fitting about being able to wander through the place you are placing your favourite memories.
- You can choose a beautiful place, your favourite place, as the container for your memories.
- It provides a nice balance between simplicity and security.

Previously in this book, I have suggested that one should use large arrays when the information to be memorised will keep growing,[31] but in this case I'm against it. You should choose a wonderful location that will snugly fit all 15 of the memories you currently want to store and no more.

[30] She had gone first, I certainly would have felt silly if I had stayed behind stood up there on my own.

[31] I would certainly hope that your list of happy memories would continue to grow.

When you find you have another dozen memories you want to add, you can find a new location and add them. Again and again. I favour this approach because the memories I wanted to store at 25, and the place I choose to store them, are very much the choices of a 25 year old, and it's nice to look at them in that context, and then look separately at the set I built up a few years later when living in London, and then again the set I built up after falling in love and having children.[32] Each location feels like it has its own wonderful personality, and I make a point of visiting them in person whenever I find myself back in an old area.

Before I start, I go and visit the location a few times and take photographs - I wouldn't normally do this for a section of my memory palace, but I enjoy this part very much and it's nice to prepare the ground properly. I then go and visualise the memories in person - again, I wouldn't normally do this. It's important to note that I'm not trying to store every detail of the moment, I'm storing just enough of a clue that my brain can pull the rest up. So my visual link for jumping off the bridge is the sudden coldness, darkness, and the panic in case the water wasn't deep enough.[33] I don't include any of the other details because I know I can bring those to mind as soon as I think of that day.

You will find that this is one of the easiest memory exercises you do. Partly because you aren't storing anything new, you are organising existing memories, and partly be-

[32]Notably, my 25 year old self had started writing this book.

[33]Very shortly afterwards I started to panic that the water was too deep.

cause the memories you are organising are likely to be extremely strong ones in their own right, with lots of evocative keywords to lock into. You also find that you review this structure more regularly, because, well, it's fun to do, especially when you feel you want a bit of a pick-me-up.

## 4.10 Summary

This chapter has introduced the idea of arrays as a memory device. The key points are:

1. The Method of Loci, first-letter mnemonics, and the Peg System are all different types of array.

2. An array can be based on anything you know well that has an order.

3. Old buildings are better for the Method of Loci than new ones because there is more going on.

4. Arrays can be open or closed, although in practice 'open' means that there is enough space for the set to grow, or that there will be enough space if it is needed (For example, I'm happy to believe that the number of Batman films will grow faster than the number of OPEC countries).

5. Arrays can mechanically generate intermediate keywords (in this chapter we used the Major System and letter pairs in separate examples) that make it easier to create the links.

6. Arrays are resilient.

7. Arrays can be connected to linked lists (and often are): in the next chapter you will see that they also contain classes. However, it's rare that a linked list will contain arrays.

# Chapter 5

# Classes

This chapter covers the advantages, disadvantages and effectiveness of the *class* memory structure.

Classes are useful when you want to remember a fixed list of properties for each item within a group of similar items. As such, you would only use them for quite large sets of information and they need careful planning.

Like skip lists, classes appear nowhere else in the memory literature.

Classes allow you to link three or more keywords in one image, however they are only useful when you are storing information about several similar examples: a class is useful when you want store the price, fuel efficiency, and safety rating for each car in a set of 20, but not when you want to memorise every detail about one particular car.

There are four examples in this chapter: Section 5.1 shows the basic operation of a class and Section 5.2 gives a larger and more practical example using inventions.

Section 5.3 expands the inventions example and shows how you would include a subclass for programming languages. Section 5.4 is a large example that goes step by step through the process of memorising a table of detailed accounting information.

## 5.1 People at a party

Consider that you are going to a wedding and want to memorise the names and occupations of the 25 or so new people that you don't already know using photos provided by the groom.[1]

The first photo is Doug. Doug is a baker so you imagine him with a spade through his head,[2] and carrying an warm loaf of bread. You then look at a photo of Pete who makes jam, and imagine him carrying some peat while raspberry jam drips down his face.

Shortly afterwards you predictably refer to Pete as James (Jam-es) or assume Doug is a gardener, or possibly both. This is because you've broken a key rule of memory: never link one keyword to two others. There are two problems with this:

1. We saw in Section 3.1.1 that one link can dominate another. When links dominate you might remember Doug's name correctly but forget what he does.

2. This example shows another problem: you can get confused about the structure of your information.

[1] Don't do this; it makes my skin crawl and I don't think I'm the only one.

[2] This is another excellent reason not to do this.

I would solve this by making a rule: for this wedding, I will remember what a person's name is by using their face as the key image for a link, and I will remember what a person's job is by using their hands as the key image for a link. I'm no longer making two links from one key object (Doug's appearance → the name Doug, and Doug's appearance → Baker), I'm making two seperate links from two seperate key objects (Doug's face → the name Doug, and Doug's hands → Baker).

So, the image we created for Doug can stay because it already matches my rule, but the one for Pete now has him throwing up peat and leaving massive sticky, jammy, handprints all over the nice clean wedding finery. Now you won't get confused about which link tells you the name and which one tells you the occupation.

As the examples get more complicated there will be more rules. Rather than say 'the set of rules we use to attach multiple links to a single key image' I use the term *class*.[3]

The class for this example would be:

Person (from photograph)

- Name →
- Job →

Our *Person* is holding/interacting with an item that links to their *job* and their face is linking to their *name*

You could think of a class as a short array: the source keywords for the array are 'job' and 'name', and the links

[3]You could use template, or, if you enjoy old-school computer science, structure or record.

are 'job → holding → ...' and 'name → face → ...'.[4]

However, a class is used differently from an array. In practice, the major difference is that you will be asking for information by label ('What is the name of this person?') rather than location ('What is the 6th member of this list?'), but there are a wide range of others.

This example introduced a class. We'll now use classes to memorise slightly more complex (and useful) information.

## 5.2 Inventors

Consider that you have a list of inventions[5] and want to remember the inventor, the year of invention and the location for each. The first eight on the list are:

- Henry Fairfield Osborn named the Tyrannosaurus Rex in 1906 in Manhattan.
- James Hargreaves invented the Spinning Jenny in 1764 in Stanhill, Oswaldtwistle.
- Guido van Rossum released Python in 1991 working at CWI in the Netherlands.
- Trevor Erskine ran the team that designed the Ford Fiesta in Cologne, which was released in 1976.

[4] This isn't *that* far away from what the computer does internally when a programmer uses a class construct.

[5] I include products, concepts and discoveries, and I picked examples that each stretch definition in their own way.

- Sheikh Mujibur Rahman was the founding father of Bangladesh in 1971.

- Pink Lady Apples were bred by John Cripps in 1973 at the Western Australia Department of Agriculture.

- Spider-Man: Into the Spider-Verse was written and produced by Phil Lord and Christopher Miller in 2018 and was made in Vancouver.

- The Hawthorne Effect was discovered by Henry A. Landsberger in 1958 in a factory in Illinois.

I've decided to use a class for this example and I've created the following template:

Invention

- Next Invention →
- Inventor →
- Year →
- Place →

The Invention is being interacted with by *inventor*, who is holding a *year* and who is located in *location*. The invention itself is later destroyed by *Next Invention*

The attachment points within a class should be very distinct. Make sure that it is hard to confuse any two of them. In the example above, it was probably an error to have 'interacting with' and 'holding' because they could be confused easily. Certainly linking, say, the left hand

and the right hand of a person to different keywords will cause problems quickly.

Our first link (using the class above) is:

> Tyrannosaurus Rex → Henry Osborn, 1906, Manhattan, Spinning Jenny
>
> ---
>
> I see the T-Rex chase scene from Jurassic Park,[6]except that the car is occupied by Norman Osborn (who, in this link, is being played by Henry Cavil), also known as Spider-Man's archenemy Green Goblin. Osborn is throwing new bombs - except that these are actually gospels (The first few letters make 906 in the Major System). When the dinosaur bites at the gospels they explode into a shower of pages, but the dinosaur is still eating them up like a dog getting thrown treats as he gets closer and closer to the truck. The truck is swerving as well, Osborn starts choking as the jeep drives into the middle of the pitched Manhattan battle from the climax of *The Avengers (2012)*. As it does, I see a giant version of my friend Jenny grab the T-Rex by the tail and spin around like an Olympic hammer thrower before launching the beast into orbit.

[6]Which I went back and watched for the purpose of getting the scene right in my head, I'm stretching the definition of 'interacted with' a little to get the image to fit.

Spinning Jenny → James Hargreaves, 1764, Stanhill, Python

---

I see Roger Moore, in a clown costume sobbing (James, Ha-Grieves), looking exactly like he did in the James Bond film *Octopussy (1983).* He's sobbing because he's got his hand, well, his whole arm, stuck in a spinning jenny, and both feet stuck in molehills and it's very painful. In his other hand he's holding a chessboard with 64 squares (I can naturally remember the century) and he's trying to use it to saw off his own arm. Things get worse as a giant python bursts in and swallows the Jenny whole: you can see the shape of it distending the snakes throat as it slides down.

Python → Guido, 1991, CWI

---

I see a giant Python, which is throttling an enormous Guy Fawkes(Guido Fawkes is the pen name of a right-wing blogger), Fawkes is holding a cudgel ('991' in the Major System) and trying to wedge open the snake's mouth with it. He's also wearing headphones that are blasting 'Bonkers' by Dizzie Rascal into his ears so loudly that they bleed (Rascal was a programming language developed by CWI that I used to use.)

There are two key points I want this example to show. Firstly, classes are complex and useful for putting *big* things into the memory. As a consequence, they take more time and effort to build than the previous structures we've seen.

Secondly, this class includes a link to the next instance of the class, thus forming a linked list. Classes are only useful if you are going to be remembering a number of them, so they will always be collected in a structure. If that structure is a linked list, then the linked list's implicit links should be explicitly in the class structure to avoid one of the class links dominating the link for the linked list. Normally I'm happy for a linked list link to in anyway dominate or 'beat' the previous keyword, but I've specifically made it 'destroy' in this example. The narrower definition reduces the likelihood of confusion, but does make it slightly more work to create the link.[7]

So far, this chapter has introduced the idea of classes and shown how they can solve the issue of linking several pieces of information to one keyword. It's easy to imagine this linked list of 'inventors' expanding dramatically with whatever you are interested in.

Part of the reason to write this book was to point out to the memory community that information generally has a structure and that everything is much easier when you can match that structure in your own memory (we'll see this explicitly with trees in Chapter 6). The events chosen for the World Memory Championships, and written about in general, focus entirely on simple lists, missing out on all the rich variety of the real world.

Classes are a major tool for us in properly matching real world structures.

---

[7]It's worth rereading Section 3.1.1 after this chapter with the knowledge that a linked list is a simple example of a class.

## 5.3 Programming languages

Consider that you have created the list of inventors in the previous section and have been adding to it for years. It has grown quite long and in that list you have the following four programming languages:

- Guido van Rossum released Python in 1991 working at CWI in the Netherlands.
- James Gosling released Java in 1995 working for Sun Microsystems.
- Don Syme is the benevolent dictator for life of F#, which was released in 2005 by Microsoft.
- Ruby was released in 1995 by Yukihiro Matsumotoi in Japan.

It would be quite handy if your memory structure let you add some more information that was specific to programming languages, like:

- List of reserved words
- Licence

I can achieve that by adding an extra rule: *programming languages can use a different class as an extension.* An extension to a class[8] is a new class that builds on a previous one. In the example below, I create a new

[8]Programmers would normally use the word 'subclass' but 'extension' fits better here.

programming language class that contains the existing invention class:

Programming Language

Invention

- Next Invention →
- Inventor →
- Year →
- Place →

- Licence →
- Reserved words list →

The *invention* and *inventor* from the included class melt together to form a terrifying monster. This monster is eating *licence* and has got its foot caught in some form of *reserved words list*

When designing this extended class, I need to make sure that it doesn't interfere with any of the existing links. If I already have invention and inventor combining somewhere then I can't use this class because I'll end up thinking that the combination is part of the subclass.

To add the information, simply extend your linking image. Add everything you need to add and make sure you review it thoroughly a few times.

My link for Python looks like this:

Python → Guido, 1991, CWI, GPL, keywords

I see a giant Python, which is throttling an enormous, burning, Guy Fawkes(Guido Fawkes is the pen name of a right-wing blogger), Fawkes is holding a cudgel ('991' in the Major System) and trying to wedge open the snake's mouth with it. He's also wearing headphones that are blasting 'Bonkers' by Dizzie Rascal into his ears so loudly that they bleed (Rascal was a programming language created at CWI that I used to use)

I see the Python and Guy Fawkes start to melt and flow together, to create an enormous scaly snake-person holding a tiny version of itself (the baby version is biting its parent's finger and wearing the skin of an eggplant(egGPLant).[9]the monster's foot is caught in the sliding door of the history building of my old university, (where I have a Method of Loci array to store the keywords in the Python programming language) the doorway is charring from the heat.

If your list gets long enough, you might have separate

subclasses for films, books, or any other type of information that you want more detail on. This feature of having classes of slightly different types in the same list is something Computer Scientists call *Polymorphism.*

[9]Python is released under the 'Python' licence, which is compatible (ish, sometimes: lawyers are involved) with the GPL licence.

## 5.4 Accounts

Consider that you run a small charity and wish to be able to recall the accounts details since you formed in 2014. The relevant numbers are in Table 5.1.

| | In | Out | Profit (post tax) |
|---|---|---|---|
| 2015 | £6,845.00 | £6,200.00 | £516.00 |
| 2016 | £24,760.00 | £21,852.00 | £2,378.00 |
| 2017 | £49,150.00 | £43,129.00 | £4,816.00 |
| 2018 | £54,228.00 | £46,199.00 | £6,492.00 |
| 2019 | £47,914.00 | £37,193.00 | £10,721.00 |

Table 5.1: Charity income figures.

Consider also that you'd like to leave space for the balance sheet figures so you can add them later if you please.

This is a long example, almost a case study. We'll start by reducing down the information as far as we can, and in the process we'll use the Major System more extensively than we have before. We'll then examine and reject at least one design of class, before settling on a suitable one. In the process we'll show that you can use the Method of Loci for the inside of classes. The final design will include a class, two versions of the Method of Loci (one as an array, one as the internals of a class), and some small linked lists.

It's also totally real: these are the accounts for the charity I run. If you find yourself getting lost, skip to the summary in Section 5.4.1

I start by removing the pence, pound signs, and part of the year. Table 5.2 shows the result of that.

| | In | Out | Profit (post tax) |
|---|---|---|---|
| 5 | 6845 | 6200 | 516 |
| 6 | 24760 | 21852 | 2378 |
| 7 | 49150 | 43129 | 4816 |
| 8 | 54228 | 46199 | 6492 |
| 9 | 47914 | 37193 | 10721 |

Table 5.2: Charity income figures reduced to significant digits.

Then we can look for any patterns that might help us. The simple solution might be to put all of the numbers into the Major System and see what pops up. Table 5.3 shows the results of that: we only get a few matches to decent Major System words because most of the numbers are too long for us to find a single word that matches.

| | In | Out | Profit (post tax) |
|---|---|---|---|
| 5 | bushcraft | penises | vulpix/flops |
| 6 | 24760 | 21852 | unmatch |
| 7 | 49150 | 43129 | 4816 |
| 8 | 54228 | 46199[10] | aberdeen |
| 9 | 47914 | 37193 | 10721 |

Table 5.3: Charity income figures with potential Major System keywords.

[10]The keyword 'rebuilded' would work, but I'd likely remember

I could arbitrarily split the number strings,[11] but a better way is to think about how the information is going to be used. I recognise that when I'm thinking about this information I generally only think about it in terms of thousands ("We will raise five thousand less this year") and I only use the precise digits when talking to funders ("Yes, thirty-seven thousand, one hundred and ninety three pounds in the year-ending"). So I'd like to set this up in such a way that the regularly used information was 'closer' than the precise information. One way of doing that is to separate the numbers into thousands (the 'quick' digits') and the last three digits (the 'detail' digits). This gives Table 5.4.

| | Quick In | Detailed In | Quick Out | Detailed Out | Quick Profit | Detailed Profit |
|---|---|---|---|---|---|---|
| 5 | 6 | 845 | 6 | 200 | | 516 |
| 6 | 24 | 760 | 21 | 852 | 2 | 378 |
| 7 | 49 | 150 | 43 | 129 | 4 | 816 |
| 8 | 54 | 228 | 46 | 199 | 6 | 492 |
| 9 | 47 | 914 | 37 | 193 | 10 | 721 |

Table 5.4: Charity income figures with the thousands separated.

I can now retry the Major System on the 'detailed' section of each number. Table 5.5 shows the resulting Major System keywords.

Clearly, the Major System worked much better this

it as 'rebuilt'.

[11]Even better, I could rewrite my code to show me multiple word matches.

| | Quick In | Detailed In | Quick Out | Detailed Out | Quick Profit | Detailed Profit |
|---|---|---|---|---|---|---|
| 5 | 6 | sherif | 6 | noses | | flabby |
| 6 | 24 | octopus | 21 | chevon | 2 | match |
| 7 | 49 | elvis | 43 | calendar | 4 | chalkpit |
| 8 | 54 | cannonship | 46 | aladdin | 6 | accordion |
| 9 | 47 | gloria | 37 | leadman | 10 | toenail |

Table 5.5: Charity income table with major keywords for the smaller numbers.

time. There are two reasons for this:

- The numbers are shorter so they are more likely to match words.

- Every number in the detailed in and out columns will be exactly three digits. So I can used any word where the start matches the number. For example 'Aladdin' is 1992 in the Major System, but I can use it here for 199 because I know I only need the first few letters. This vastly increases the number of possible matches: in the wordlist that I use to generate keywords there are a little over 86 thousand words that match exactly three digits, but over 293 thousand that match three or more digits.

So far we have reduced the complex information in Table 5.1 down to a group of short numbers and Major System keywords. We can now start making a class.

My first design for the class is below. I'm going to assume that the year itself will be part of the link from a wider structure.

Financial Year

- In →
- Out →
- Profit →

A local bank has doors that are made from *in*, when I open them, I see *out* escaping through the windows while *profit* cowers in the secure area.

I like this design. I like the simplicity of the incoming coming from the entrance and spending flying out of the window. It feels nice.

This design introduced a new idea. I'm using the Method of Loci to make my template rather than a set of rules. When it's time to finally commit this to memory I'll visit five different banks and choose one bank branch for each year.

I can actually do even better than that. If I am going to visit five banks, then I may as well do it in my local high street, and if I'm going to do it in my high street then I may as well start at one end of the street, make the first bank the location for my 2015 accounts, the second the location for my 2016 accounts and so on. What I'm really doing here is creating a Method Of Loci array that links to my classes.

There's something else new here: this is the first time we are using the Method of Loci as a template for many locations, rather than being tied to one specific location. It turns out to be an extremely useful thing to do for constructing classes in general.

Before I properly commit this to memory I want to check the class out properly. I want the door to the bank to be made out of the keyword for income but when I look at Table 5.5 I see that most of the keywords are humans, and the other is an animal. 'Made out of' and 'humans' don't link together that well. Also, most of the keywords for profit are inanimate objects, so they will be harder to link to something that 'cowers in the secure area'. Lastly, I think I want to make the split between the 'quick' and 'detailed' numbers really obvious in the definition.

This the improved design:

Financial Year

- In(quick → detailed) →
- Out(quick → detailed) →
- Profit(quick → detailed) →

A local bank has doors that are guarded by *in*, when I open them, I see *out* escaping through the windows while a swarm of *profit* starts coming to life inside.

### 5.4.1 Summary of accounts example

We now have our complete class. We can explain it as follows: when I walk down my high street, I know that the first bank I see contains the accounts from our first year (2015), the second bank contains the second year and so on. Inside each bank I have an image that leads me to think of the total income for the year guarding the front, an image for the outgoings leaving by the window, and another image inside for the profit. Each of those is actually an image for just the 'thousands' part of the number - they all link to another image which encodes the details down to the last pound.

This has been a long step-by-step example that makes use of almost everything in the book so far. Once properly committed to memory, it is simple to mentally move to a particular year, get an immediate sense of the amounts involved, and be able to drill down into exact figures easily. Because we used a class, we can later extend it with options for balance sheet figures. An example might be:

Financial Year

- In(quick → detailed) →
- Out(quick → detailed) →
- Profit(quick → detailed) →
- Balance sheet total →

A local bank has doors that are guarded by *in*, when I open them, I see *out* escaping through the windows while a swarm of *profit* starts coming to life inside. The building starts shifting to one side ('balance' sheet) and as it does you become aware that an enormous *balance sheet total* is emerging from the ground.

## 5.5 Summary

At its simplest a class is a set of rules that allow you to successfully link one keyword to several more. Because you have to remember the rules themselves it's only worth doing if you are going to use them repeatedly; hence we use classes when we want to memorise lots of examples of the same type. This chapter has introduced the idea of classes as a memory device. The key points are:

1. Classes are a natural choice when you have a group of the same **type** of entity, each of which have information that is specific to them.

2. Classes are almost always used in combination with other structures, although they can form linked lists on their own.

3. Classes can be expanded later.

4. The internal structure of a class can be anything that works, from a few simple rules to a full internal Method of Loci.

5. Don't be tempted to use 'mirrored' hooks: using the left hand of a person as one hook and the right hand as another will get you in trouble fast.

6. Classes can be very large and it's worth doing iterations of your design before you commit it to memory.

# Chapter 6

# Trees

In the last chapter, you learned about classes. In this chapter you'll learn that if you design your class in a particular way, then you can connect many instances of that class into a particular structure. There are lots of possible structures, but this chapter is interested in one in particular: the tree.

Trees look like this:

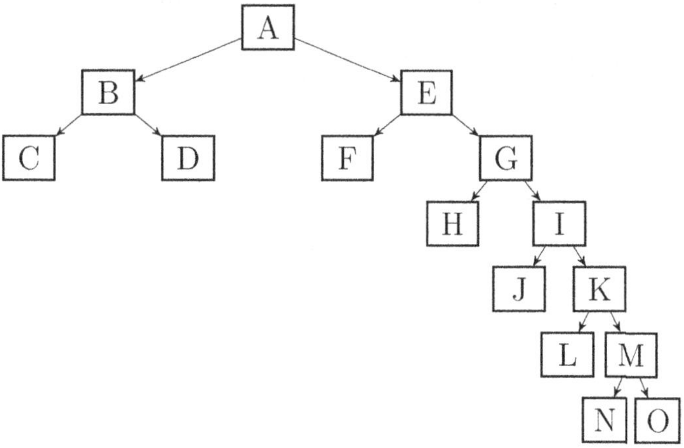

Each tree has a *root* or 'starting' node, which will be of a particular class. In the example above, the root node is labeled 'A'. The root node will be linked to up to two[1] 'child' nodes (labeled 'B' and 'E' in the diagram above), which are of the same class, and which may have child nodes of their own. There will be a direct path from the root node to any other node in the tree. When drawn out, this structure resembles the branches or roots of a tree, which is how it got its name.

**DEFINITION 7** *In general, node 'Bob' is a* child *of node 'Alice' if there is a direct link from 'Alice' to 'Bob'. If 'Bob' is a child of 'Alice' then we say 'Alice' is the* parent *of 'Bob'.*

Depending on how you are using the tree, they can be either very hard or very easy to add information to. They are also relatively hard to build, can be quite fragile, and are tiresome to review. Trees perform brilliantly in a particular set of circumstances and poorly in others. In Chapter 7 we shall meet the Karnaugh Map, which effectively works as a specialised tree (although is much easier to build and maintain).

This chapter is set up for memorists to learn about a programming concept. If you are already a programmer, you will find many of the concepts familiar[2] and you are welcome to skim such things as the in-order tree traversal.

Over the course of this book, the examples have moved from 'cover every detail of something fundamental' to

[1]Actually it can be any number, but the examples in this chapter are limited to two.

[2]You might also find them wrong: lots of oversimplifications have been necessary.

'play with the implications of a new concept' so you will find there are fewer examples of my own strange imagery and many more diagrams and numbers in this chapter. This is partly because we're moving from areas where there are well tested approaches into more experimental work, but also because structures like classes and trees aren't really useful unless the example is *big*, so it becomes increasingly difficult to cover every detail.

This chapter contains only three examples: we use the World Cup knock out stages to demonstrate the basic structure and use of a tree, I then use historical contexts of novels to show how a tree can be used to search for information, how it can become 'unbalanced', and how we can extract all the information for later review. In the final example, which uses a decision tree to identify the best local attraction to recommend to hotel guests, we deal with our largest tree so far, and look at when it's useful for a tree to be unbalanced.

## 6.1 The 2018 World Cup knockout stages

Consider wanting to memorise the results of all 15 matches in the 2018 Football World Cup knockout stages.

If you draw them out, the diagram stages of the World Cup look like Figure 6.1. In particular, they look like a (sideways) tree. The root of the tree is the World Cup final, the branches lead to the knockout matches and the 'leaves' are first set of matches in the knockout stage. You can see that the node representing the final is the

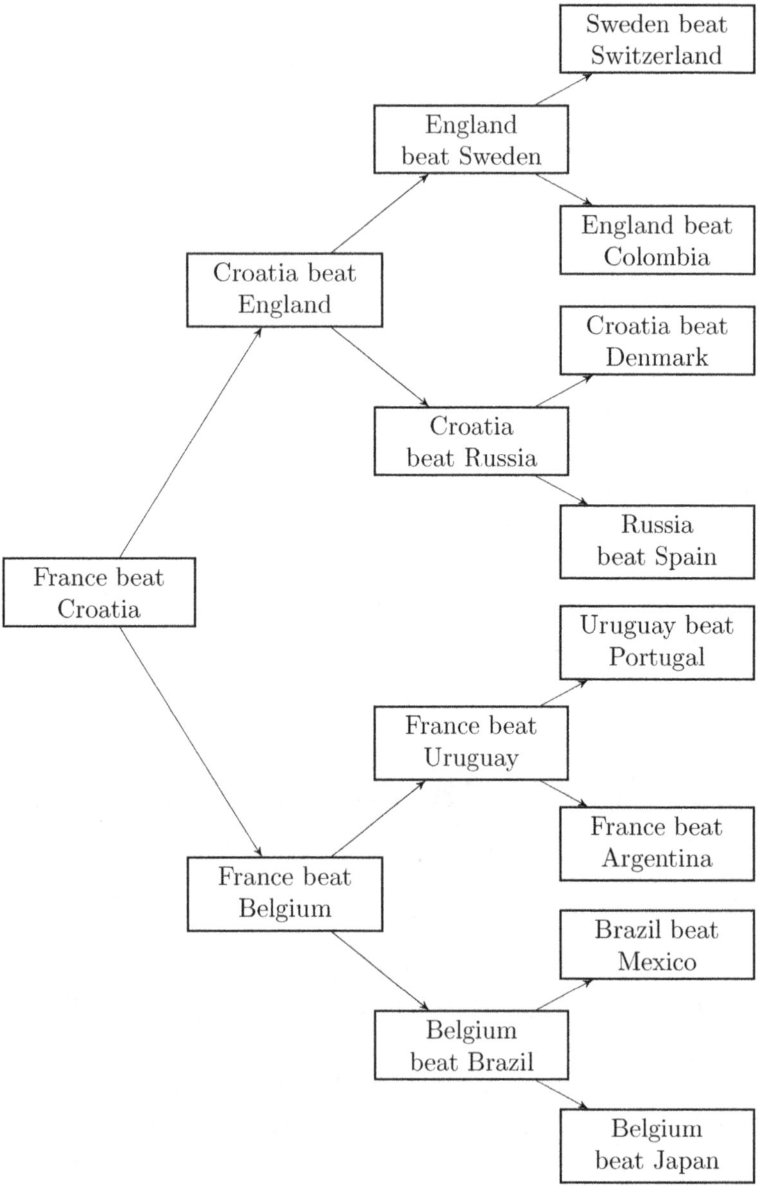


Figure 6.1: The knockout stages of the 2018 World Cup.

parent of the nodes for the semi-finals.[3] So in this tree, the match in the parent node is the same as 'the match the winner of this match played next'.

In Section 5.2 we saw that classes can form a linked list if they contain a link that points to another instance of that class. If you create a class that contains two separate links to other instances of the class, then your instances (which we shall call *nodes*) can form a tree. It follows that we should be able to build a structure that exactly matches the tree of World Cup games.

I've designed the following class:

Football Match

- Winner →
- Loser →
- Parent match[4] →

I pick a film as the backdrop of the image. The hero of the film is linked to *winner* and the villain is linked to *loser*. A character from *parent match* is chaotically inserted into one of the film's scenes.

In the previous chapter, we used bank branches with predicable structures as templates for a class, in this one we're going a little further and using films that conform to a set structure. I'm going to assign films to matches like so:

[3]And the 'grand-parent' of the quarter-final nodes, although that's not a term we'd normally use.

[4]This is 'parent' in the sense of 'parent node in tree'. In football terms it would be 'the next match the winner played'.

1. (France beat Croatia) will use *The Empire Strikes Back*

2. (France beat Belgium) will use *Robin Hood: Prince of Thieves*

3. (Croatia beat England) will use *Terminator 2*

4. (England beat Sweden) will use *Austin Powers*

5. (Croatia beat Russia) will use *The Princess Bride*

6. (France beat Uruguay) will use *Die Hard*

7. (Belgium beat Brazil) will use *Lion King*

8. (Sweden beat Switzerland) will use *Wolf of Wall Street*

9. (England beat Columbia) will use *Casino Royale*

10. (Croatia beat Denmark) will use *Hamilton*

11. (Russia beat Spain) will use *Top Gun*

12. (Uruguay beat Portugal) will use *Bridget Jones's Diary*

13. (France beat Argentina) will use *Frozen*

14. (Brazil beat Mexico) will use *Clue*

15. (Belgium beat Japan) will use *Star Trek Into Darkness*

I'm starting with the 'root' of the tree, which is the France-Croatia match, and creating the following link:

| Empire Strikes Back $\rightarrow$ France beat Croatia |
| --- |
| I see Luke Skywalker and Darth Vader dueling climatically in cloud city, except Luke's Lightsabre is now a glowing French rendering and Vader's trademark black armour is now a chessboard pattern (Croatia is the only national team to play in checks). There is no parent match in this example. |

Both France and Croatia beat teams in the semi-final so I'm going to create the following links:

| Terminator 2 $\rightarrow$ Croatia beat England |
| --- |
| I see Darth Vader (representing the *parent match*) arriving in 1992 Los Angeles where he uses the force to lift both Terminators off the ground, rendering them useless until he can work out what has happened. Instead of bike leathers, T-800 is wearing a cravat (which were invented in Croatia) and the T-1000 is a literal pile of 1,000 tea bags with tiny screaming faces. |

| Robin Hood Prince of Thieves → France beat Belgium |
|---|
| I see Luke Skywalker arriving at the climatic battle between the Merry Men and the castle guards. A castle guard engages him in a comical sword fight, which goes badly as his sword keeps having bits chopped off it. Meanwhile, Robin Hood is at the Sheriff's mercy, until he pulls a miniature Eiffel Tower out of his boot and stabs the Sheriff (who looks exactly like Poirot, the great Belgian detective) through the heart. |

Now, let's take a moment to look at the three matches so far. I start at the root and can easily recall that France beat Croatia, but I can also ask the question "What other film did Luke end up in?" to find what match France played before this one, and I can ask "What other film did Darth Vader end up in?" to find out what match the loser played before this one. This is unusual: if the class formed a linked list we would only be able to go in one direction from the start, here we can go in two.

I'm going to add some more links.

| Austin Powers → England beat Sweden |
|---|
| I see the liquid metal robot T-1000 oiling into Austin's HQ. Austin tries his classic 'Judo Chop' to no avail and runs manically through the base throwing items at the robot until he finally escapes. In the final confrontation, Austin is stripped to his Union Flag underpants while Dr Evil dances to Abba. |

Princess Bride → Croatia beat Russia

I see Schwarzenegger's T-800 land in a swamp. The robot is swiftly attacked by some unusually large rodents, but deals with them swiftly on account of his massive strength. In the climatic confrontation, Westly is lying on a four poster bed, except the posts have been replaced by Tesla coils, so electricity is arcing all around (Nikola Tesla was born in (modern) Croatia). His nemesis, Prince Humperdick (who looks exactly like Vladimir Putin) looks on enraged.

Die Hard → France beat Uruguay

I see the heroic John McClane about to run over glass shards in his bare feet when Robin Hood improbably swings by on a rope and sweeps the detective off his feet. In the climatic confrontation, McClane is dressed as Napoleon and his nemesis Hans Gruber survives being thrown off the building by turning into a bird (one of the possible origins for the name of 'Uruguay' is linked to the birds on the river), rendering the whole ending rather silly.

| Lion King → Belgium beat Brazil |
|---|
| I see the Sheriff of Nottingham appear in the middle of a pack of lions, and immediately be mauled to death. In the climatic fight, the villain Scar starts using capoeira but is defeated by Simba throwing an enormous Brussels sprout at him. |

The root node has two matches as child nodes[5], and also each of those two matches have two matches as child nodes.

Now, I start at the root and can easily recall that France beat Croatia, I then ask the question "What other film did did the hero end up in?" to find what match France played before this one. I follow the link to Robin Hood, and recall that France beat Belgium. I can again ask "What other film did the hero of this film end up in?" to be lead to *Die Hard* and discover that France beat Uruguay. I can navigate to any other part of the structure by asking the following questions:

- What other film did the hero of this film end up in? (Who did the winner play before this?)

- What other film did the villain of this film end up in? (Who did the loser play before this?)

- What character is in this scene that isn't in the original film? (Who did the winner go on to play?)

[5] We would often say 'as children'.

Equally I could ask different questions and end up in any other part of the structure.

Every node in this structure lets you choose two routes away from it (three if you include going back towards the root node). That is the defining characteristic of a tree.

Once you have finished building the tree, you find that it's a more natural structure for this sort of information. It's easy to describe a team's journey through the tournament by following links, which is much harder with a linked list of all the matches.

Although the tree structure makes it easy to answer any individual question about the data, it makes it quite hard to *recite* it all.[6] It can be done (See Section 6.2.1) but I suggest that you draw trees out on paper to review, rather than try and recite them: even the simple tree in this example is hard to keep track of. Section 6.2.1 goes into some detail on how to properly go through all of the nodes in a tree.

This example was intended to show the basic structure of a tree and indicate how to move around it. The key points are that the tree has a root, and that root will generally be your starting point. It's a relatively weak example: many people would find it as easy to sit down and learn the original results. However, this example is here to set the scene for later, more powerful, ones. We'll return to the World Cup in Section 6.4.

---

[6] Thus making it quite unsuitable for memory competitions.

## 6.2 Historical context of books

Consider that you, an avid reader of historical fiction, would like to memorise the years that your books are set. You also want to know which books are near a particular year so that when someone tells you that a particular bridge was built in 1844, you can think 'ah, that's before *Jane Eyre* but after *the Gold bug*' and thus have a bit more sense of the time period. Finally, you want to be able to add new books to this structure as you read them at a rate of maybe one a week.

These are the starting books:

1. 1939 - *The Book Thief*
2. 1940 - *The Lion, the Witch and the Wardrobe*
3. 1976 - *Life of Pi*
4. 1944 - *Gravity's Rainbow*
5. 1855 - *The Great Train Robbery*
6. 1782 - *Ross Poldark*
7. 1823 - *The Revenant*
8. 1775 - *A Tale of Two Cities*
9. 1664 - *Girl with a Pearl Earring*

We'll then add the following books:

1. 1327 - *The Name of the Rose*

2. 1500 - *Wolf Hall*

3. 1805 - *War and Peace*

This presents a problem: linked lists and arrays can cope with both sorted data (satisfying the second criteria) and adding additional information (satisfying the third criteria) but they are unable to do both at once.

However, we can build a tree that stays in sorted order when we add new information. One such tree is shown in Figure 6.2.

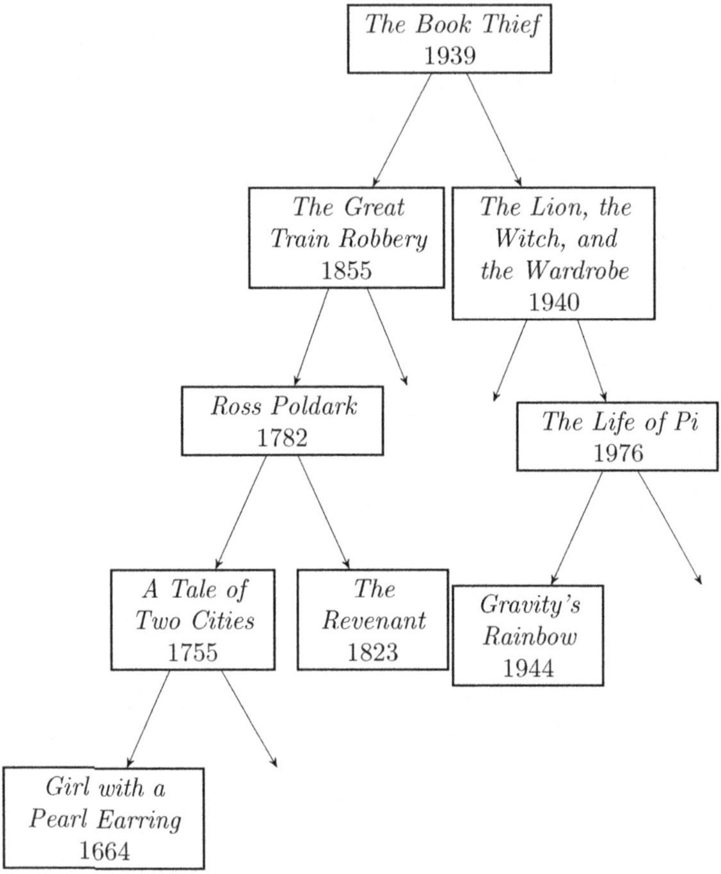


Figure 6.2: A tree that shows books in setting order.

The tree in Figure 6.2 is built according to a set rule: child nodes to the left have to be set before their parent node, and child nodes to the right have to be set after their parent node. Take a minute to check that this is correct for Figure 6.2. There are many different ways that we could have constructed this tree with those books,[7] this is one example, you'll see another shortly.

Assume you have recently been watching *Hamilton* and are wondering about books set in the same time as the 1800 election. Using Figure 6.2 you know you want before *The Book Thief* so you take the left branch. *The Great Train Robbery* is 55 years too late so you again take the left branch to find *Ross Poldark* which is 18 years before. Now you take the right branch to find *The Revenant* and the tree ends. When you are finished, you know that the two closest books in your structure are *Ross Poldark* and *The Revenant*. If were prepared to cast your net a little wider, you could follow the close branches.

### 6.2.1 Converting the tree into an ordered list

It's possible to look at this tree and then write out the names of all the books in setting order. The process is a little tricky to get one's head around but it's reasonable when you get the hang of it.[8]

[7]There are 4,862 unique correct possible trees for this example according to members of my board gaming group, which possibly explains why I very rarely beat them.

[8]This process is strictly for converting from an *ordered* tree into a ordered list. If you don't care about order or if you are happy to

The process is this: for any node, write out the contents of the nodes to its left, then its own contents, then the contents of the node to its right.

So for Figure 6.2 we start at at the node for *The Book Thief* and proceed as follows.

- The node for *The Book Thief*, has a left subtree, so we must process that first.

- The node to the left is *The Great Train Robbery*, and before we can process that node, we must process its own left subtree.

- The node to the left is *Ross Poldark*, and before we can process that node, we must process its own left subtree.

- The node to the left is *A Tale of Two Cities*, and before we can process that node, we must process its own left subtree.

- The node to the left is *Girl with a Pearl Earring*, which doesn't have any child nodes, so we can write out *Girl with a Pearl Earring* on our paper.

- We now go back to *A Tale of Two Cities*. Its left subtree has been processed so we can process this node and write *A Tale of Two Cities* on our paper. It doesn't have a right subtree so this node is done.

- We now go back to *Ross Poldark*. Its left subtree has been processed so we can process this node and

draw the tree, then there are much easier ways.

write *Ross Poldark* on our paper. This node has a right subtree so we have to process that before leaving.

- The node to the right is *The Revenant*, which doesn't have any child nodes, so we can now write out *The Revenant* on our paper.
- We now go back to *The Great Train Robbery*. Its left subtree has been processed so we can process this node and write *The Great Train Robbery* on our paper. It doesn't have a right subtree so this node is done.
- We now go back to *The Book Thief*. Its left subtree has been processed so we can process this node and write *The Book Thief* on our paper. This node has a right subtree so we have to process that before leaving.
- The node to the right is *The Lion, the Witch, and the Wardrobe*. It doesn't have a left subtree, so we can process this node and write *The Lion, the Witch, and the Wardrobe* on our paper. This node has a right subtree so we have to process that before leaving.
- The node to the right is *The Life of Pi* and before we can process that node, we must process its own left subtree.
- The node to the left is *Gravity's Rainbow*, which doesn't have any child nodes, so we can write out *Gravity's Rainbow* on our paper.

- We now go back to *The Life of Pi.* Its left subtree has been processed so we can process this node and write *The Life of Pi* on our paper. It doesn't have a right subtree so this node is done.

- We return to *The Lion, the Witch, and the Wardrobe*, which is now completely processed, and then to *The Book Thief*, which is also completely processed, so we can stop.

Writing out that whole process for a small tree took three pages. I promise you it is quite simple on paper once you get the knack, but remains fairly difficult to do in your head.

### 6.2.2 Balanced trees

The tree in Figure 6.2 is effective, but a lot of the nodes are much further from the root of the tree than they need to be. In fact, the whole section from *The Book Thief* to *Gravity's Rainbow* acts like a small linked list. In computer science we say that this tree is *unbalanced.*

**DEFINITION 8** *An* unbalanced *tree is one where there is a large difference in length between the shortest path from the root to a leaf, and the longest path from the root to a leaf.*

Now look at Figure 6.3. Twice as many books can be reached with only two links than in the previous tree, and every book can be reached with three links. Programmers would call the second type of tree *balanced.*

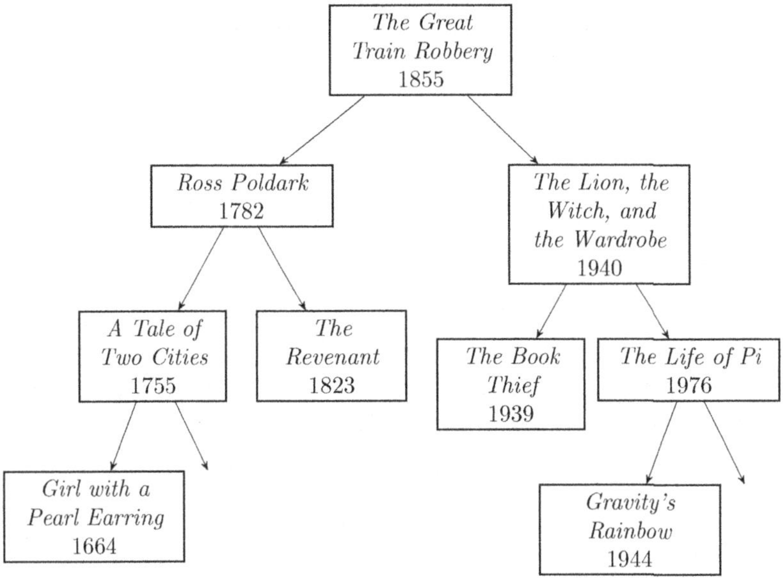


Figure 6.3: A balanced version of a tree that sorts into setting order

Both Figure 6.1 from the World Cup example and Figure 6.3 are balanced, which means that each of the routes from the top of the tree to the bottom are roughly the same length. Every path from the winner to the start in the World Cup tree consists of exactly four matches and the tree looks very even.

For the remainder of this example, we'll use the balanced version of the book tree because it's faster to use and has fewer potential dead ends.

Trees being unbalanced is totally fine when modeling unbalanced data, and I'll later show you cases where you want an unbalanced tree on purpose, but in general try to balance trees where possible.

### 6.2.3 Creating the class

This example started on page 136; we've spent a lot of time since then talking about the theory of tree data-structures and how they can be used. It's now time to actually create the structure and show some example links.

Here's the class I'm going to use:

> Book Setting
>
> - Year →
> - Before →
> - After →
>
> Using the book itself as the basis of the instance. The key object of the narrative or title is linked to *year*, a character from *before* appears in an early scene and a character from *after* appears in a late scene.

The above template is similar to the one we used for football matches, although here we can use the novel's own narrative as the setting, which makes everything simpler. I'm only going to include a couple of examples, partly for space but also because these examples are particularly unhelpful if you haven't read the books.

The Great Train Robbery → 1855, Ross Poldark, The Lion The Witch and The Wardrobe

---

I see a train, but it's a fake train, it's made up entirely of 55-gallon drums! Everything from the wheels to the whistle is made of drums, it looks like one of those enormous Lego structures. I see Ross Poldark, as played by Aidan Turner, being thrown from the train in the opening sequence, and I see the film's[9] final opening of the two safes interrupted when one turns out to contain a large angry lion, and the other turns out to contain a larger, angrier, witch.

The Lion, the Witch, and the Wardrobe → 1940, The Book Thief, The Life Of Pi

---

I see a wardrobe that has been tipped over to use as a very small stage for a rock concert. Bowling For Soup are playing the line I've never quite understood from that song they did when I was young. All I remember is that it's about a 40. I see Death (the narrator of the *The Book Thief*, but I see him in is Discworld persona) leaning against the iconic lamppost. Later I see Aslan, the eponymous Lion, sitting next to Richard Parker, the tiger from *The Life Of Pi* awkwardly in a lift.

I decided I don't need to store the first couple of digits

[9] I admit I haven't read the book and am basing this on the film. I feel quite the fraud.

of the year for books of the last three hundred years or so because I'll likely remember that from the general feel of the book.

The structure of a sorted tree lets me be a little more sure about the year for many of the books anyway. In Figure 6.3 I know that *Gravity's Rainbow* is definitely set after 1940 and before 1976 because of its position in the tree.[10]

### 6.2.4 Adding books to our tree

Recall that one of the requirements our structure had to satisfy was the ability to add new books and maintain the order (otherwise we could have used a linked list or an array). Specifically we were asked to be able to add the following books:

1. 1327 - *The Name of the Rose*

2. 1500 - *Wolf Hall*

3. 1805 - *War and Peace*

Starting with our balanced tree from Figure 6.3, and using our rule of 'earlier settings to the left and later settings to the right', there is only one place to put *The Name of the Rose*: it uses the left branch of *Girl with a Pearl Earring*. *Wolf Hall* then uses the right branch of *The Name of the Rose* and *War and Peace* uses the left branch of *The Revenant*.

[10]The fact that it is set during the second world war will also give me something of a clue...

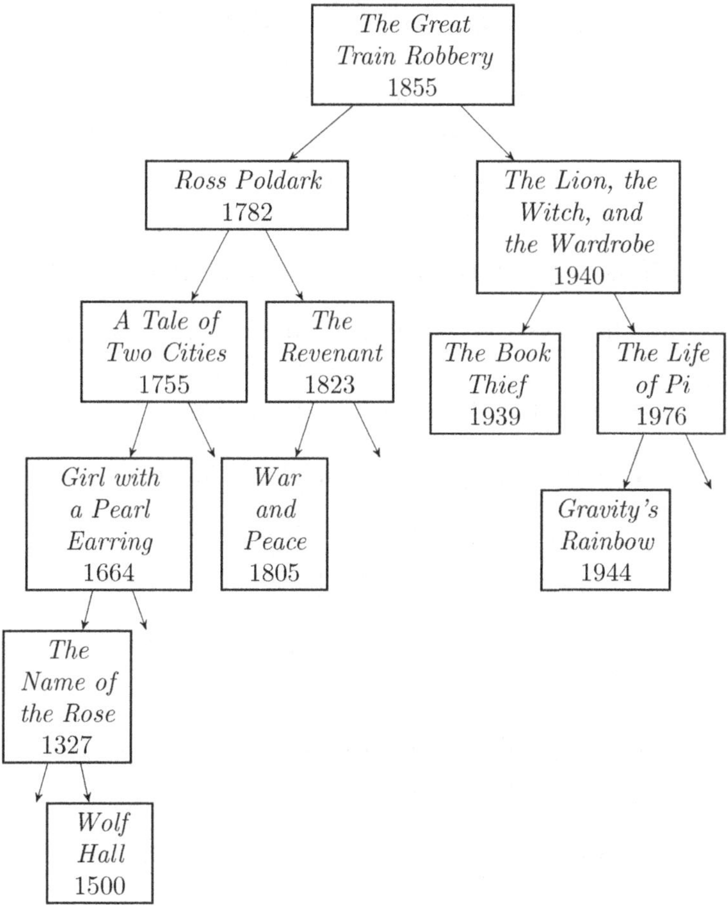


Figure 6.4: Our book settings tree with the final books added.

Check for yourself that our tree remains in order and that our requirements are entirely satisfied. The final tree is shown in Figure 6.4, you'll note that it is now slightly unbalanced. This is entirely normal - in computer science there are many processes for 'rebalancing' trees, but they would be unhelpful for our purposes. If you find yourself suffering as a result of a *dramatically* unbalanced tree, then the best option might be to start again from scratch.

### 6.2.5 Summary of book context example

This has been a very long example. In it we:

- Introduced the idea of a tree that is always sorted
- Showed how trees could be balanced or unbalanced
- Demonstrated how to use the tree to find years that were 'close' to a target year.
- Demonstrated how to extract all of the contents in order of year.
- Covered adding additional books to the tree in such a way that order was maintained.
- Showed a new way of creating links by using the narrative structure of the book itself.

So far we've now looked at trees for information that is inherently tree-shaped like the World Cup, and we have shown that we can use trees keep inherently linear information in order. We're next going to look at a more common example of a tree based structure, the decision tree, and in the process learn why we don't always want a balanced tree.

## 6.3 Conversational tree

Consider that you work at the reception in an expensive hotel and guests frequently come to you to ask for 'something to do'. There are over a hundred local attractions but you don't want to keep recommending the same ones, nor do you want to work down a list of a hundred activities with guests who say 'no' to each one. In fact, you are sure that your guests would get grumpy at more than five questions. You'd like a series of questions to carefully divide the available options.

This is a natural use case for a tree. Classically, a tree's main advantage over a linked list is that it's much much faster to find the thing you are looking for. For example, if you have a linked list of 64 objects, you will on average need to follow 32 links to find the one you want, and in 10% of cases you'll need to follow over 55 of them. By contrast, searching a (balanced) tree of 64 items will *never* need you to follow more than five links, because every link you follow contains only half the remaining nodes.

Now, the above is only true if the tree is in some sense ordered. The World Cup tree wasn't ordered, but we can build a tree of potential activities that is. I'm going to talk about how to memorise that tree, but we are going to draw it out first.

Let's consider a fairly obvious question for a seaside hotel "Do you like water based activities?". If we make that first question our 'root', then our next job is to sort the 100 activities into ones that involve the water and those that don't. For simplicity, we'll assume it's a 50-50 split. As long as we make sure that those activities stay on the correct side of the tree, it will work as a search tree. If we add some more questions like: "Do you have children?" and "Are you interested in food?" and keep sorting the activities, we'll shortly end up with a tree that looks like Figure 6.5.

Figure 6.5 only has room for 32 or so activities, but it's easy to imagine continuing to build this structure on paper until every path of five questions leads to a suitable activity or two that we can memorise. The actual construction of this example is left as an exercise.

Don't worry too much about balance when building a decision tree. Sometimes you want an unbalanced tree. For example, if you knew that the hotel's famous Jazz lounge was the major attraction and that 80% of people loved it, then you'd want to be able to identify that in fewer steps and you'd accept some unbalancing to do that.

Other applications for decision trees include:

- A salesperson's conversation. Done well, this is a smooth conversation that the customer thinks is naturally flowing, while they are actually being guided though a conversational tree in which the salesperson has a response prepared for the natural answers to each question (and if you give a new answer, that will be added to the tree for the next customer).

- A doctor's questions - doctors have to check for a bunch of important symptoms and if a red flag is raised they have to follow it up quickly. This is absolutely a tree structure.

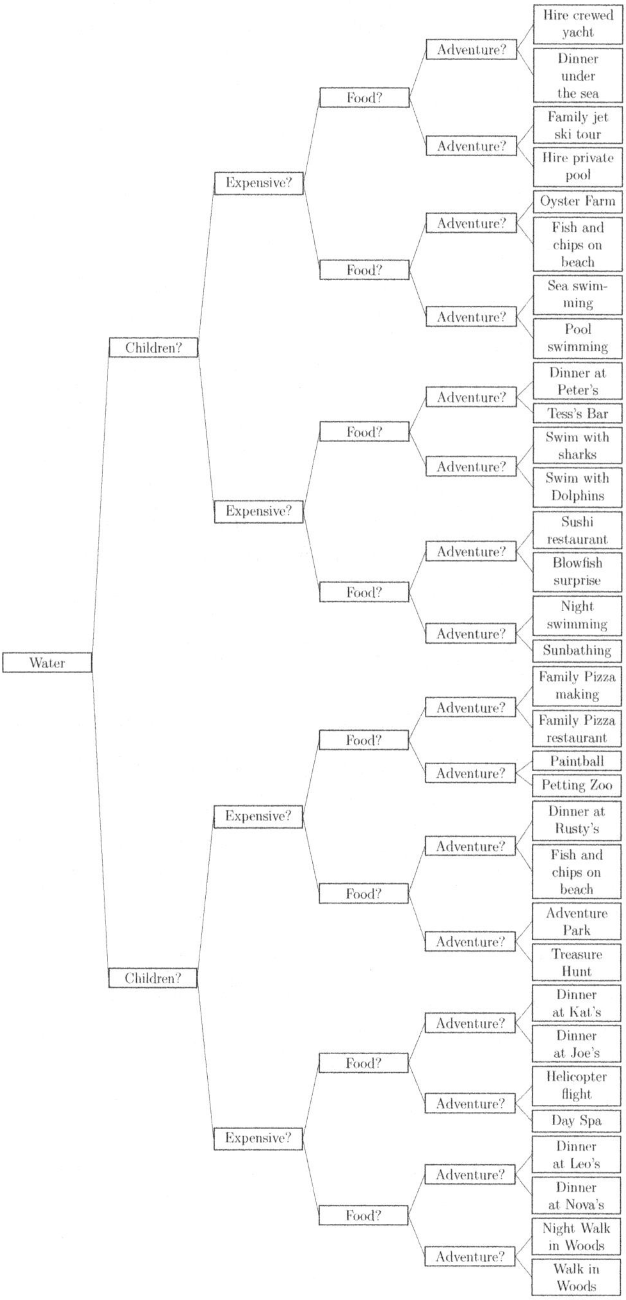


Figure 6.5: Hotel activity decision tree, up branches are taken for 'yes', and down branches are taken for 'no'.

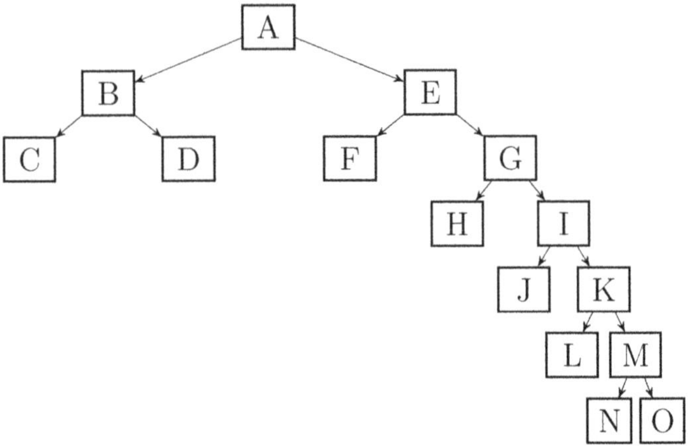


Figure 6.6: An unbalanced tree: the path from A to C is two links long but the path A to N is six links long.

## 6.4 World Cup (again)

Consider that you again want to memorise the results of all 15 matches in the 2018 Football World Cup knockout stages.

The approach described in the previous section was very general, but if your tree is completely balanced[11] there is another approach.

Consider the tree in Figure 6.7. It is numbered left to right, then top down. It has the interesting property that if you know the number of a node, you can work out the numbers of its child nodes. The left child can be found by doubling the parent's number, and the right

[11]It doesn't have to be *completely* balanced, but you can waste a lot of space using even a slightly unbalanced tree.

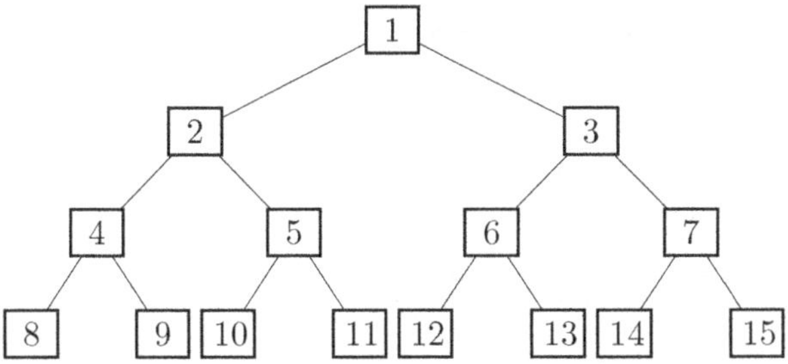


Figure 6.7: A tree that can be compressed to an array.

child can be found by doubling and adding one. You can also work out the parent of the node by halving the number and discarding any remainder. Take a moment with Figure 6.7 to confirm:

1. That you can move around the tree in this way

2. That all the numbers from 1 to 15 are accounted for without any gaps.

Now I put the list of matches into a particular array:

1. → (France beat Croatia)

2. → (France beat Belgium)

3. → (Croatia beat England)

4. → (France beat Uruguay)

5. → (Belgium beat Brazil)

6. → (Croatia beat Russia)

7. → (England beat Sweden)
8. → (France beat Argentina)
9. → (Uruguay beat Portugal)
10. → (Belgium beat Japan)
11. → (Brazil beat Mexico)
12. → (Russia beat Spain)
13. → (Croatia beat Denmark)
14. → (England beat Columbia)
15. → (Sweden beat Switzerland)

This array matches the numbers 1-15 to the 15 matches. This array has the same property as the tree: you can find the previous match of the winner by doubling the match number, and the previous match of the losing team by doubling and adding one. We've compressed the entire tree from Section 6.1 into an array.

This has lots of advantages:

- An array is vastly easier and quicker to build than a tree.
- An array is a lot more resilient to change than a tree.
- It's very quick to write out the array as a tree on paper.

It also has a few disadvantages:

- Having to keep converting back to numbers and then double or halve them really slows you down when you are trying to traverse the tree. That's okay for tree shaped information, or when you are going to be able to draw out the tree on a scrap bit of paper during an exam, but I suspect it would be tricky for a decision tree or for magicians using it as part of an act.

- This works best with balanced trees. If, like in Figure 6.8, you have a tree that is perfectly balanced except that one node is missing, then you can put it into an array and leave one gap in the array. But if you have a tree that is perfectly balanced except for one additional node (like in Figure 6.9), then you will end up with an array that has almost as many gaps as links and that will be a massive waste of time, space, and energy.

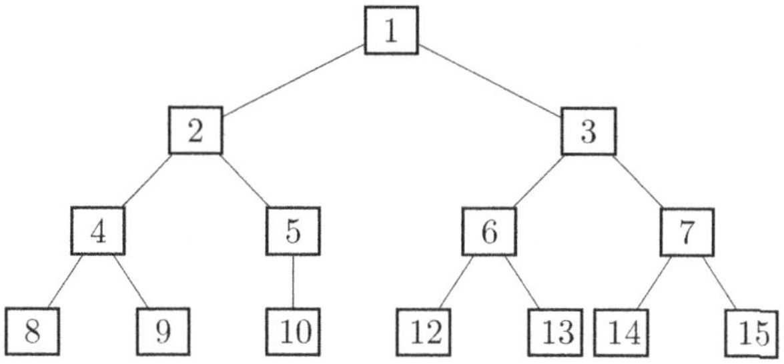


Figure 6.8: A slightly unbalanced tree that can still be reasonably compressed to an array.

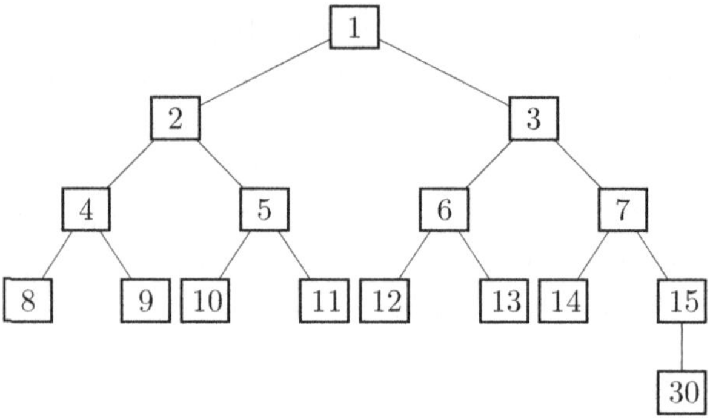


Figure 6.9: A slightly unbalanced tree that should not be compressed to an array.

## 6.5 Family trees

Consider a family tree such as the one in Figure 6.10, you have two parents and each of your parents has two parents and so on. This is a natural structure for a tree: it is hard to imagine a linked list or array successfully coping with more than a couple of generations.

However, while the techniques in this chapter will work perfectly for Figure 6.10, they won't work in general for family trees because in general, family trees aren't trees. As soon as someone has more than one child[12] the information stops being tree-shaped and starts being a *graph*.[13][14]

[12]Not to mention instances where someone has more than one partner, marries a second cousin, or when a pair of siblings marries a different pair of siblings.

[13]All trees are graphs, but not all graphs are trees.

[14]Readers might have noticed that I didn't include the 3rd place

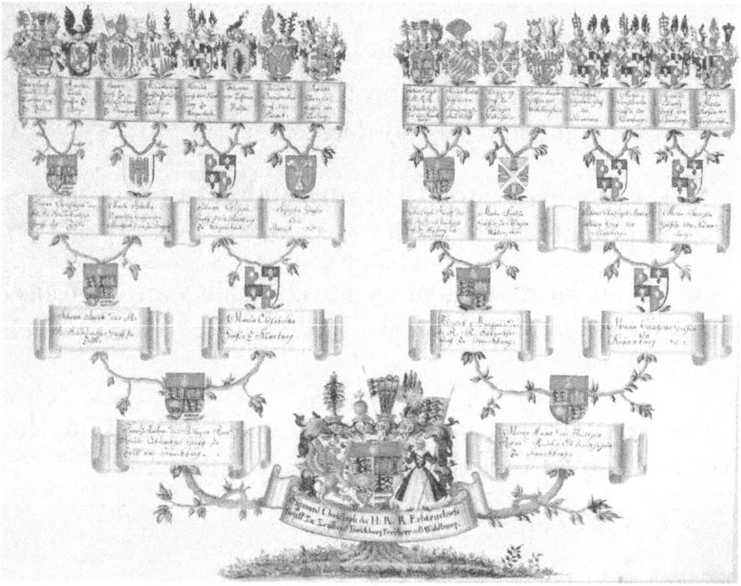

Figure 6.10: The family tree of Sigmund Christoph von Waldburg-Zeil-Trauchburg, which also happens to be a perfectly balanced binary tree [Wikipedia, 2020].

There isn't space in this book to properly cover graphs as a memory structure,[15] this example is here to get you to think about the limits of the technique. You are welcome to consider effective techniques for dealing with family trees in particular, and then graphs in general. Some particular examples that require a graph to solve:

- Given a country, what other countries does it have land borders with, and then, which *other* countries do those countries border?
- the names of roads in an random area of central London.
- Given an ingredient, what cocktails can it be used in and what are the other ingredients in those cocktails?[16]

By comparison, some examples of information that are tree shaped but also monstrously large are:

- Chess openings
- Poker draw calculations
- The Dewey decimal system[17]
- Taxonomic hierarchy

playoff game in the World Cup tree for this reason.

[15]Also, I haven't explored it in anything like the detail I'd need to feel confident about telling other people.

[16]The novel *The Rosie Project* by Graeme Simsion (a former database designer himself) has a scene in which the main character has chosen the wrong structure for this problem. The character then rebuilds a new structure *on the fly* during a brief hesitation.

[17]This is a purposely unbalanced tree: there are some

## 6.6 World Cup Yet Again!

Consider that you yet again want to memorise the results of all 15 matches in the 2018 Football World Cup knock-out stages. However, this time, you happen to know your own ancestor tree perfectly until your great grandparents.

Since you already know one tree, you can link each member of your family tree to a match in the World Cup tree and build a tree-to-tree array. This has the same advantages and disadvantages as compressing a tree into an array, but is slightly easier when you have a well known tree to hand.

## 6.7 Summary

This chapter has introduced trees as a memory device. The key points are:

1. A node in a tree is similar to a node in a linked list, except the tree links to *two* next nodes rather than one.

2. Every node in a tree is a class.

3. Trees are naturally suited to information that is already tree-shaped: tournaments, decision trees, flowcharts.

---

quite short codes and then there is the 23-digit monster for 'Arab Attitudes Toward Israel' by Yehoshafat Harkabi, which is 301.15433012917492705694. [Kahn, ]

4. If you are modeling fixed unbalanced data, then it's cool if your tree is unbalanced, but it's also good to try and balance a tree before you memorise it.

5. Balanced trees can be compactly encoded into an array.

6. Trees that you know well can be linked to trees that you are learning as part of a tree-to-tree array, as long as they have exactly the same structure.

# Chapter 7

# Karnaugh Maps

This chapter introduces Karnaugh Maps and I agonised over it because a Karnaugh Map isn't a Computer Science Data Structure in the normal sense. A real Karnaugh Map never enters a computer: it's something you draw to simplify a circuit and certainly most working programmers would struggle to remember what one was. However, it is useful from a memory perspective and so I have included it.

A Karnaugh Map is a special method of arranging an array in such a way that subsets of information are easy to find.

Karnaugh Maps might need several practice goes before they click for you, I certainly needed a few goes when I was introduced to them.

## 7.1 Banned Classics

Consider that you want to commit to memory a list of classic novels that were historically banned. You are interested in bans that happened in both the United States and the United Kingdom, and would like to be able to distinguish which.

You could have three lists: books banned only in the US, books banned only in the UK, and books banned in both. That's perfectly reasonable.

You could also use a Method of Loci array, and assign regions. You would make a rule that 'everything that is on this side of the room was banned in the US, everything on the other side was banned in the UK, and everything in-between was banned in both'.

The first option appears more flexible because you can add information at the end of the lists more easily.[1]

However, having separate lists has problems with scale. If we say that you now wish to remember the books banned in Ireland, the UK, and the US, then we would need eight lists, which starts to become unwieldy.[2]

The Method of Loci can cope much better with three countries. Taking a park as an example location, we would nominate the centre as the region we place the books banned in all countries, then nominate three locations around the edge as the region we place the books banned in each country, and then, quite naturally, the

[1]Technically you would have a problem if a book that is already banned in one location is then banned in another, but most book banning is historical, so that's unlikely to happen.

[2]We could use a decision tree to organise them reasonably well, but that has issues that we'll discuss later in this chapter.

area between two countries would contain the books banned in those, but not the third.

In practice, such an array would be quite time-consuming to construct and I suspect it would be a little unreliable, but it would function.

The purpose of this example is to demonstrate that we can use the Method of Loci to distinguish between items in a list that have different attributes. The next example will show that we can do this in a much more systematic and reliable way by using a Karnaugh Map.

## 7.2 Restaurant menu

Consider you are a server at a restaurant that has a menu of eight items. The restaurant wants to make sure that they cater to a variety of food needs so it makes sure they include vegan, gluten-free, and nut-free options. Indeed, they go as far as to make sure that they have one meal for every combination of those three options - so there is an option that is vegan, gluten-free and includes nuts, and there is an option that is gluten-free, nut-free, but isn't vegan.

Consider that you wish to include a structure in your memory palace that includes all the these meals and allows you to easily answer questions like:

- Can you tell me all your gluten-free options?
- Which options are vegan and include nuts?
- What is the option that has nuts, gluten and isn't vegan?

- Does the nut roast have nuts in it?[3]

In short, you might be asked any question about any combination of attributes of the menu or an item on it.

Now, this is Chapter 7, so we've seen a range of structures that we could use. We could use three linked lists:

1. Vegan → Salad → Buffalo Cauliflower sub → nut roast with potatoes → Bulgar Wheat with walnuts and tomato
2. Nut-free → Salad → Buffalo Cauliflower sub → Beef Chilli → Ham Sandwich
3. Gluten-free → Salad → Beef Chilli → Nut roast with potatoes → Egg and Almond salad

That works, but it will be a faff to answer complex questions 'Okay, I've got the list of nut-free dishes, I now have to check every item on the list to see if it's on the gluten free list'. That will take a really long time and use up a lot of working memory.

Or we could use an array with some attached links:

1. Salad → vegan → nut-free → gluten-free
2. Buffalo Cauliflower sub → vegan → nut-free
3. Beef Chilli → nut-free → gluten-free
4. Ham Sandwich → nut-free

[3] If you think this is a far-fetched question then you've never worked in a restaurant.

5. Nut roast with potatoes → vegan → gluten-free
6. Bulgar Wheat with walnuts and tomato → vegan
7. Egg and Almond Salad → gluten-free
8. Egg and Almond Sandwich

That's a lot better because you are iterating over one set, rather than three, but it's still taking a while.[4]

Another approach would be to build a decision tree, like the one in Figure 7.1. That makes it a lot easier to answer questions about specific food groups, but runs into trouble if people ask questions about the wrong level of the tree: it's hard to answer 'Which of these dishes are gluten-free?' easily.

None of these structures are entirely satisfactory for eight items, and they certainly wouldn't be for 16, 32 or 64 items. You could manage by using two of them at once, but it would be nice if there was an easier way.

There is. We're first going to use the main room of the restaurant to set up an eight item Method of Loci array. We're going to use the corners of the restaurant[5] as our eight hooks, four of them at the corners of the ceiling and four of them at the corners of the floor.

Next, I write out what Computer Scientists would call the 'truth table' of the menu. Table 7.1 shows every food and is clear which attributes it has.[6]

I'm now going to stand in the main room of the restaurant, just in front of the main entrance. I'm going to look

[4]In practice, the array example is a lot easier to build than this because it's pretty easy to remember that, for example, the beef chilli isn't vegan and the nut roast contains nuts, but it's still slow

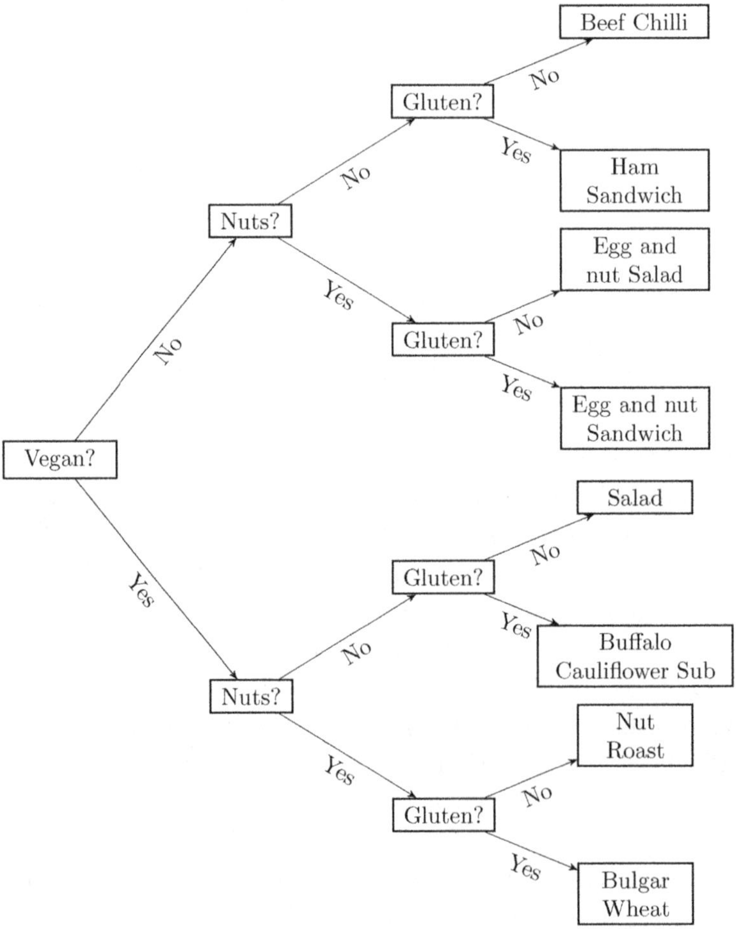


Figure 7.1: A decision tree for the menu in Section 7.2.

| Nut-free | Vegan | Gluten-free | Meal |
|---|---|---|---|
| Yes | Yes | Yes | Salad |
| Yes | Yes | No | Buffalo Cauliflower sub |
| Yes | No | Yes | Beef Chilli |
| Yes | No | No | Ham Sandwich |
| No | Yes | Yes | Nut roast with potatoes |
| No | Yes | No | Bulgar Wheat with walnuts and tomato |
| No | No | Yes | Egg and Almond Salad[7] |
| No | No | No | Egg and Almond Sandwich |

Table 7.1: Restaurant menu truth table.

at the ceiling and I'm going to call that my vegan ceiling. I'll do whatever link I need to make sure that stays in my head (by definition, the floor will be the non-vegan floor). I'm then going to label the wall opposite the entrance the nut wall (so the wall with the entrance in it is the nut-free wall). There are two walls remaining so I'll call the one to my left the gluten wall and the one to my right the gluten free wall.

I now look at my list. The first option is 'Salad' and I find the corner of the room that is made up of the vegan ceiling, the nut-free wall, and the gluten-free wall. I should find that by looking up and over my right shoulder and I create my linking image in that corner. The second option is the Buffalo Cauliflower sub, which I place in the corner above my left shoulder. The Beef chili is down and

---

to search.

[5]I'm assuming that the room is rectangular.

[6]It's ordered in descending order of the binary number you get when you put the attributes together, which is a hallmark of a traditional truth table.

to my right and the Ham Sandwich is down and to my left. The rest of the meal follows in the same way - the next two items (which are both vegan and contain nuts), go into the corners of the ceiling of the wall in front of me and so on.

Now, all of our questions are easy to answer - if I want to know the nut-free options on the menu I look at the corners of the wall by the entrance. If I want to know the items that are vegan and gluten free I look at the two places that the ceiling meets the wall to the right.

This structure has been set up in such a way as to allow one to quickly look at subsets of information based on criteria. It has three advantages over a decision tree:

- It's faster and easier to build.
- It doesn't matter what order the questions are asked in.
- You don't have to ask all the questions, you can ask only a couple and get all the relevant responses.

It has also got some disadvantages compared to a decision tree.

- It is only really effective for balanced trees.
- It gets hard to build particularly large structures of this type.

We call this structure a *Karnaugh Map* This structure can be used for medical decision trees ('The patient has low blood pressure, elevated glucose, and is drowsy, what are the actions we should take from here?'), or indeed, any situation where we sort information by attribute.

## 7.3 A bigger menu

Consider that the restaurant owner has decided to include spicy dishes as well. There are now 16 options for any combination of vegan, nut, gluten, and spice preferences.

We can rebuild our Karnaugh Map so that it fits this situation. This time I'm going to find four hooks on each wall, one on each quarter of the wall. That means that if I hold my hand in the exact centre of the room, there should be eight hooks above it, and eight below it. In fact, there should be eight hooks in front of it, behind it, to the left of it, and to the right of it.

Once I have my hooks, I'm going to nominate two adjacent[8] walls as my 'nutty' walls and two as my 'spicy' walls - it's important that one wall ends up being in both of these, so you end up with a shared wall and a wall that is neither spicy or nutty. I'm then going to call everything below the middle of the room the vegan section. Lastly I'm going to pick two opposite corners of the room as my 'gluten' corners.

Once I've done all that there will be exactly one hook for every possible combination of vegan, nut, gluten, and spice preference, and it's a relatively simple matter to add the links for the menu items.

That is a four-element Karnaugh Map - there are designs for five and even six element ones but I haven't tested them.

The key value of a Karnaugh Map is in memorising overlapping sets. Broadly, if you can represent something as a Venn Diagram, you can use a Karnaugh Map to

[8]They don't really have to be adjacent, but it helps me.

effectively memorise it

With the techniques you now have, you could reasonably and easily use a Karnaugh Map to memorise the contents of Figure 7.2 (hint, you want a three criteria Karnaugh map and some linked lists).

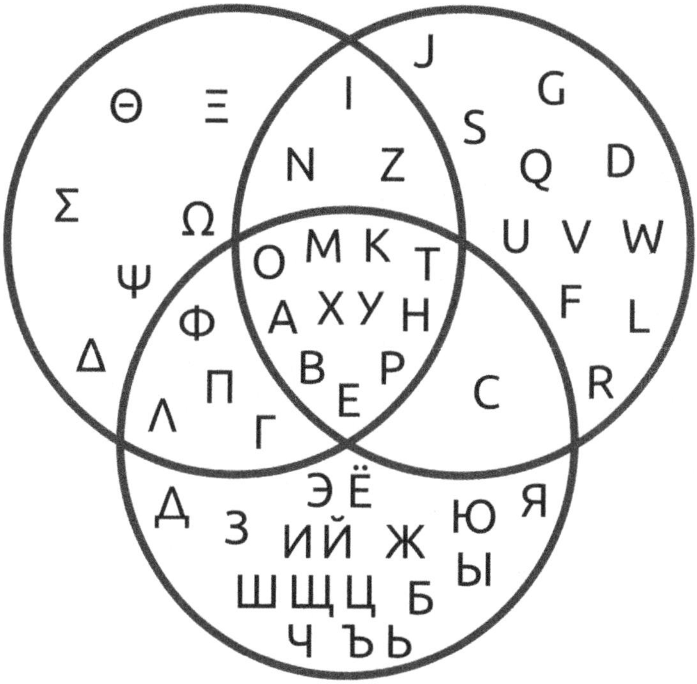


Figure 7.2: Venn diagram showing the uppercase glyphs shared by the Greek, Latin, and Cyrillic alphabets.

# Chapter 8

# The Palace

This chapter covers (finally) building your memory palace. One of the themes of the first chapter was to try and reclaim the idea of the memory palace from a pop culture magic superpower and re-establish it as an actual useful tool. Having established that a memory palace is 'literally just a list' this chapter talks about how one might get started.

There are three examples in this chapter. The first discusses picking a central structure for your memory palace, the second introduces the idea of substructures and the third covers making alterations to an existing memory palace. I very much define a 'good' memory palace as 'one that is easy to review' and so much of the content in this chapter is implicitly about reviews, which we deal with much more explicitly in the next chapter.

This chapter also starts the final third of the book, which is a general discussion of memory palaces and their uses. This third is much less prescriptive and has a general feel of 'I do it this way, but whatever works for you'.

## 8.1 Organising multiple structures

Consider you have 20 or so sets of information memorised.

1. The countries of OPEC.
2. The stations on the London Underground Circle Line.
3. Matches of the 2018 World Cup.
4. The voice cast for the film *Hotel Transylvania 3: Summer Vacation*

...

16. Your national insurance number
17. Your partner's mobile phone number
18. Dose information for Co-codamol
19. Bus timetable information.

At some point in the next ten years one of those pieces of information will become vitally important to your life or career. You don't know which one in advance. However, you also know that over time some of the links, no matter how well you lock them into your head, will fade or break down. What should you do?

The answer is simple: you should review the links. To review them, you need a reasonable and ordered way of working through them so that you know nothing has been missed in your review. What you need in fact, is an ordered list of links to each of the data structures you already have.

Congratulations! You've just invented the memory palace. Recall from Chapter 1 that a memory palace is:

**DEFINITION 1** *A* memory palace *is a memorised list of other information you have memorised.*

The first action to take is to pick a structure for your central list. If you are going very 'classical'[1] then you will build a Method of Loci array based on a familiar place. I personally use an array based on the periodic table, so I link Hydrogen to a poem I memorised, carbon to my National Insurance number and oxygen to a list of rugby positions.

If your memory palace is subject specific, then you can, somewhat comically, learn the syllabus and then use that as a starting point. For example, if your whole memory palace was built around GCSE chemistry, then you might have the following basic structure (note that the natural and artificial links are the opposite way around than you would normally expect).

1. $\rightarrow$ Atomic structure $\Longrightarrow$ (your information about atomic structure)

2. $\rightarrow$ the periodic table $\Longrightarrow$ (your periodic table array)

[1]By which I mean, 'expected by the cultural gestalt' rather than 'the most common approach in a survey'

3. $\rightarrow$ chemical bonds $\Longrightarrow$ (the three chemical bonds)
4. $\rightarrow$ structure and bonding of carbon $\Longrightarrow$ (your information about carbon)

This approach has the advantage of making the review quite reassuring; you are proving to yourself that you know everything on the syllabus.

In general, I would recommend that you choose an array as your central list. You want to be able to iterate through it easily so a tree would be unsuitable and a linked list feels too fragile, particularly as it gets larger.

Once you have chosen your array, fill it up exactly as you would any other array. Don't leave spaces for things you are 'going to remember', it will simply bug you every time you review it.[2] Finally, don't start constructing a memory palace until you have at least ten things to put in it.

## 8.2 Building a flexible structure

Consider that you want to construct your first memory palace out of the dozen or so structures you already have, but you are worried about doing it 'wrong' and making some mistakes permanent.

Currently your list of structures is:

- Nobel Prize Winners
- Average temperature per country in the UN

[2]I was very happy to slot 'countries of OPEC' into a gap when writing this book.

- Population of every country in the UN
- Family Birthdays
- Booker Prize Winners
- The names of the 282 known Stradivarius violins.
- Numberplates of family cars.
- Trees of Great Britain and Ireland and their leaf shapes.
- Events in the Life of John Keats
- Recipes

You are already regretting not putting the temperature and population information into a class structure. You're worried that if you commit this list to memory then you will have problems later on.

I would tell you be relaxed about the structure at this stage. Just throw everything in. An untidy structure is far better than one that never gets built (I have two separate 'nice memories' lists in my main structure that are nowhere near each other).

However, you can also use sublists. In the previous example I mentioned that I link Helium to a particular poem as the first element in my memory palace. My next entry, Hydrogen, is to a sublist, which I notionally label 'programming', which contains sets of reserved words for various languages and will have more added in the future. I also have sublists for 'book quotes' and 'London underground lines' because those happen to be natural for me.

Here's the first few elements of my memory structure.

1. $\Longrightarrow$ Helium $\rightarrow$ The Rudyard Kipling Poem If.

2. $\Longrightarrow$ Hydrogen $\rightarrow$ Programming $\Longrightarrow$ (reserved words in the Java programming language, reserved words in Python)

3. $\Longrightarrow$ Lithium $\rightarrow$ A set of nice memories.

4. $\Longrightarrow$ Beryllium $\rightarrow$ Religious quotes $\Longrightarrow$ (references from the Bible, Quran and Vedas, each with their own structure)

5. $\Longrightarrow$ Boron $\rightarrow$ The set of countries in OPEC.

6. ...

It's important to note - my overall structure is an explicit list, and the Java, Python, Bible, Quran and Vedas structures are all explicit lists, but they aren't actually explicitly connected. I have a direct link to 'programming' but from there I don't need an explicit list to remind me which programming languages I know. I also don't need an explicit list to remind me of the world's three largest religions. The purpose of the memory palace is to give you just enough information to review everything else you've memorised. Chapter 9 goes into much more detail on reviewing.

Obviously, if I was memorising the number of adherents of the 22 religions on the Wikipedia page for religious populations, then I *would* have a very explicit structure for that, and I would use it to explicitly link to the relevant holy texts. However, I use just enough structure that reviewing is easy.

So, it's quite possible that you want this grouping:

- Winners
  - Nobel Prize Winners
  - Booker Prize Winners
- Things I had to learn at University
  - Average temperature per country in the UN
  - Population of every country in the UN
  - Events in the Life of John Keats
- Family
  - Family Birthdays
  - Numberplates of family cars.
- Recipes
- The names of the 282 known Stradivarius violins.
- Trees of Great Britain and Ireland and their leaf shapes.

It's also quite possible that you only need to properly memorise the six main items on the list because the sublists will be obvious on review.

## 8.3 Altering your memory palace later

Consider that you have a simple memory palace. The root of your palace is an array that maps between the novels of Terry Pratchett and your other structures. Let's say that the first few links in the structure are:

1. The Colour of Magic → A linked list of inflation in the UK by year
2. The Light Fantastic → A full array of laws concerning inheritance
3. Equal Rites → Speeches of Martin Luther King
4. ...

...and the government has just voted to accept a new law on inheritance. This is a problem for you because you have no room in your array for it. How do you fit it in?

There are several options:

Firstly you can start an entirely new structure and link a different bit of your memory palace to it, which would give you something like this:

1. The Colour of Magic → A linked list of inflation in the UK by year
2. The Light Fantastic → A full array of laws concerning inheritance
3. Equal Rites → Speeches of Martin Luther King

4. ...
37. Making Money → A new linked list of inheritance laws

This has the advantage of simplicity, even if it is slightly untidy and might take you a while to get from one to the other. If the reason you have memorised the inheritance laws is because you want to be able to quote the details of any given law, then this is fine. However, if you have memorised them because your job occasionally requires you to be able to recite them all, then this is less good.

Secondly, if you are sure this will be the only addition, you can add the new law at the first available slot and add a link back:

- The Colour of Magic → A linked list of inflation in the UK by year
- The Light Fantastic → A full array of laws concerning inheritance
- Equal Rites → Speeches of Martin Luther King
- ...
- Making Money → new inheritance law → the inheritance array

That means that two rooms in your memory palace take you to the array, but one of them includes some additional information. This only really works if you work through your memory palace 'backwards' when you review; looking at the most recent addition first. There's nothing wrong with that, and it's probably worth considering as a default for exactly this reason, but it's not entirely natural (and if you are using a tree, quite hard to do).

The third, is to build a new memory palace. This sounds drastic, but it's worth thinking about because you are really only rebuilding the central structure. Although there might be 100s or 1,000s of bits of information that you can access from it, the central structure itself is only 37 links long. Moreover, very sadly, the current structure will run out of space quite soon because Pratchett no longer writes novels. When you rebuild using a different array, you can reorder the whole sequence, put the inheritance laws next to each other, and also organise every other element and leave space for growth. A complete redesign isn't something I'd suggest to do on a regular basis, but I can certainly imagine doing it once after five years of throwing all sorts of information into a central structure that wasn't quite designed right.

## 8.4 Summary

This short chapter has discussed choosing the central list for your memory palace. It has repeated, over and over again, that the purpose of the memory palace is to allow periodic reviewing and that you should choose a central structure that makes that as easy as possible.

# Chapter 9

# Maintenance: How to ensure that your structure is safe

Chapter 1 made clear a fundamental belief that runs through the book: memories fade, and the only way to ensure they are reliable is to review them regularly. This chapter covers how I do that review. It is written with slightly less authority than the early chapters because this isn't an area where I have tested out multiple approaches or researched or consulted widely: it's 'How I do it'.

This chapter covers reviewing and restoring and what the difference is. It covers keeping a hard copy, and about what happens when you leave your palace to rot for a few years.

## 9.1 Hard copy

You should keep a hard copy of your memory palace.[1]

This sounds silly - surely the whole point of a memory palace is that you don't need a hard copy?

Actually, a hard copy comes in extremely handy. It can be used by friends or partners to quiz you, and it also turns out to be quite useful on those odd occasions that something goes wrong.

Your hard copy should be a list of all of the keywords you are storing and should include some way of showing which keywords are linked to each other. Don't store the links themselves; they are exhausting to write, and if you are happy to write them down then you probably haven't made them ridiculously memorable enough.[2]

As it happens, the very exercise of writing out your hard copy is an example of reviewing, which I talk about in the next section.

## 9.2 Reviewing and restoring

I, and anyone with a memory palace, could sit down with a stack of paper and write out every bit of data we hold in our heads. It would take a while and a few sheets of paper, but it would be relatively rapid and the only thing slowing us down would be our writing speed. After we had done it we would feel confident that we understood

[1]Obviously I don't mean 'hard' - I use a digital document.

[2]I have some problems recalling the examples in this very book. It turns out that when I was writing them for you I didn't make them as ridiculously embarrassing as I would have for myself.

how well our memory was working and that, by the act of following those links, we had made them stronger, much like regularly walking on a patch of grass eventually wears a path.

That's reviewing. It's something we should do regularly.

Here's something else I can do. I can sit quietly somewhere and I can work through my memory palace. For every link I can ask myself a set of questions. What does this smell like? What does this image sound like? What are the tiny details? I can visualise the image as completely as possible. This takes longer, and requires a bit more effort and imagination. It's also a *much* better way of making sure that your memory palace is in full working condition.

That's restoring.

I've done a restore about three times in the last decade. I've never done the whole palace at once, and it's normally been as part of some repair on a part of the palace that had stopped working. When I've been restoring, I've found having the hard copy *very* useful, largely because I've generally left it too late, so I'll be working with a section that has 40% good links, 40% fading links that want restoring and 20% entirely broken links that I need to lookup and then rebuild.

The point here is that memory structures degrade over time, and they will eventually detach from each other and 'float' off into the deep sea that is your mind. However, this is preventable - all you have to do is to bear in mind maintenance when you construct each link and then do a bit of maintenance every now and again.

## 9.3 How often should I review?

You will need to review regularly, but 'regularly' depends on a lot of factors. If you have built a lot of redundancy into your images (Section 2.1) or if the memory palace is small, or if you are using it on a very regular basis, then reviews can be far apart. If it is complex, rarely used and made in a hurry, then you'll need to review it more regularly.

My advice: start with three months. If, after three months, you can perfectly recite everything without any trouble, then leave it longer next time. If you really struggle, then either do reviews more regularly, or take the time to do a decent restore now and build it back stronger. You'll gradually find the right time period based on how tolerant you are to the occasional mistake.

My preference is to pick a section and review it while I'm drifting off to sleep. This is a terrible approach[3] because I'm incentivised to pick sections I know well, I'm unlikely to reach the end of any long chains without falling asleep, and if I find a broken link then I'm unlikely to do much about it. Train journeys and boring meetings are much better and [Brown, 2007] mentions using the back of a taxi.

## 9.4 Disaster recovery

Consider that your reasonably large memory palace has fallen into disuse and that most of a decade has gone

[3]Although it is an excellent way to drift off to sleep.

past since you last made any effort to maintain it. This in fact is exactly what happened to me. I started writing this book in 2012 and stopped partly because I had, for personal growth reasons, made a conscious effort not to be 'smart' and so I turned away from fact retention as a worthwhile goal.

In the years that followed, I did a lot of work on myself to remove some of my less social habits and eventually came full circle. In 2012 I started this book as a know-it-all academic but in 2021 I finished it as a father and as someone who runs a business and it is useful to know the absolutely correct figures for our accounts, or indeed the names and preferences of the rather worryingly large number of people that appear to know my children. Hence I started metaphorically blowing the dust off the furniture of my memory palace. Some bits were fairly well maintained - I'd got a lot of use out of the room where I had stored 15 of my favourite memories for example, but quite a lot of it was crumbling around me. As you might expect, I set to putting it to rights.

My hard copy told me that I had about 560 keywords in my structure at the time, and so I sat down and worked on rebuilding them. There were lots of surprises - things I had forgotten that I'd memorised but that were working perfectly when I was reminded, and things that I thought were locked tight but that were very much falling apart. Some links just needed a bit of revitalising, and some had gone entirely and had to be replaced with completely new images. It actually took not much more than a couple of hours because the hard work had been in coming up with the link in the first place, rather than working through the visuals and making sure to tick off the five senses that I was using.

The first 10 sections of my memory palace contain 166 pieces of information[4] and it took me 90 or so minutes to write them out in full. Much of the 90 minutes was spent fixing broken links. The second time I did it, a week later, it took 20 minutes and had far fewer links to fix. A week later it took 10 minutes flawlessly. I don't have timings for the remaining sections of the palace, but the main point is this: even after years, the vast majority of information was still there, needing only a small bit of work to bring it back to life.

## 9.5 Summary

This chapter discussed maintenance of a memory palace. The key points were:

- There is a substantial difference between reviewing and restoring and both are important.

- You should keep a hard copy of the set of keywords in your memory palace.

- Without maintenance, your palace will gradually fail, but it can be brought back quite quickly.

[4]The pieces are of varying complexity, some are only keywords, others are phone numbers, national insurance numbers, lines of poetry, page references and so on.

# Chapter 10

# Conclusion

The first half of this conclusion will cover the same topics as the introduction, but quite differently. The introduction was designed to make sense to people who hadn't read the book, but this chapter is designed to give some context to the people who have. The second half of the chapter is more reflective, and covers the external forces that shaped the book, the material that was cut out, and the material I would have liked to include.

So, you now know about memory palaces. You understand their purpose - they exist only to make it easier for you to review their contents. You know how to construct sections quickly, how to make sections of your palace very sturdy and reliable or how to make sections give up their information quickly. You know what questions to ask yourself beforehand to help you choose.

It's worth noting that this has been a book about *advanced* memory palaces rather than *big* memory palaces. Size is largely a function of persistence in this area, and that's not something I can teach. However, I can make sure that you build on solid foundations.

You might be looking forward to using these techniques to pass some exams, or regretting not doing it for previous exams, because then you'd be able to remember some of the content now. But I hope you are broadly satisfied with the outcome.

I do appreciate that my approach to the subject differs radically from some other authors. That's one reason why I keep suggesting that this is the second book you read on the topic. I am certainly more cynical about some aspects, although I flatter myself that I'm also more hopeful in places. I hope that this book might have jolted a few people out of comfortable modes of thinking, and am prepared to endure any number of angry reviews complaining that I put their beloved Method of Loci in the same section as childhood mnemonics for planets.

I made several promises in the start of this book, and this seems to be a good time to check in on them.

I promised to put existing memory techniques into a data-focused framework. I'm happy to say I did this, although mostly this was achieved when I named the chapters after the computer science structures. When I started the book I had dreams of showing readers how to calculate sizes of their palace, how to work out the entropy of information, and how to think about the amount of steps needed to retrieve any part of the information. Much of this content was cut when it became apparent that it was a bad idea to try and teach two topics at once, but I like to think that the concepts are baked into the very DNA of the book.

I promised to include new structures that were never before seen in memory textbooks: trees, classes, skip lists, and Karnaugh maps. When I set out to write the book I thought I would include more, but these four (or, more accurately, combinations of these four) turn out to be enough to cover 99% of cases that aren't covered by existing memory structures.

I promised to include a lot of anecdotal information about my own memory palace, and I think this is the criteria I came closest to failure on. It's certainly true that I regularly noted when something was *outside* my experience, and I added quite a lot of notes on how I prefer to work, but I didn't explicitly link the notes to my own examples until the final chapters. It's quite possible that the correct approach would have been to create an entirely new, tidy, and well-ordered memory palace specifically for the book, and then describe its features, but I think that would have ended up being a different book. As it is, much of the educational value of this book is when it points out my errors.

I'm very proud of the book, but there are a lot of places where this book fell short of my ambitions and I think it's only fair to you that I talk about that.

- I would have liked to write about shared memory palaces, both in the sense of making use of other people's work and creating them together. I think there is a lot to be said for the use of shared mnemonics in training and education.

- I would have loved to have built a memory palace specifically for this book and that was much cleaner and clearer than my existing one. I wanted to pick a topic that was large enough to show the power (like a chemistry A-level, perhaps) and that could be useful in its own right.

- I would have liked to have had an entire chapter on emotion and memory. The 'Good Things' list is a starting point and I feel like there is a lot more to say on the general topic. It may well turn into a book in its own right.

- I would have liked a chapter on temporary information, but it was never going to happen. Partly because this is a book about permanent storage, partly because it's an area that's a bit more crowded (because of memory competitions and the like) and partly because I haven't proven my ideas to my own satisfaction let alone anybody else's.

In addition, quite large sections got cut. Some of the cuts were obvious: I wrote a long rant about memory palaces in fiction that would have been filler at best, I disposed of a number of very long examples, and I was very happy to cut a fair amount of motivation text when I rewrote the book as 'the second memory book you should read'. Some of them were quite hard: I removed a section I quite liked on classes that was, on reflection, me arguing on my own. In total about 45 pages were cut after being drafted and countless other ideas or concepts got removed in earlier stages.

The most significant cut was on the topic of entropy. I had a chapter on entropy as a concept and its application to both information in general and memory techniques in particular, and it would have served to cement the intellectual case for the work and show concepts that underpin everything else in the book. Some general references to the idea are scattered through the text, but I originally wanted to foreground it quite heavily: it's one of the key things that I think about when I am structuring memories. It got dropped partly because the tone of the book shifted away from it, and partly because I found it difficult to articulate - it was like a native English speaker explaining the grammar of English. I follow all the rules but I can't explain them.

As a result of that cut, I also cut out a chapter on lookup tables (in the Computer Science sense) that talked about, for example, how much easier it is to memorise a numberplate if you know the structure, or how much easier it is to memorise chemical formulas when you know the Hill System. It was a nice chapter but it really needed the entropy work to come first.

I know the book is better as a result, but do think these are important topics that I should return to.

## 10.1 Other books I have written or am writing

I wrote the first version of this book three years ago. Since then I've started to write a lot more, if you'd like to know more about follow up books, then please visit this part of my personal homepage.

## 10.2 Calls to action

I leave you with some concrete actions you can take right away.

- Get into the Bingo Caller habit from Section 2.2 and never let a naked number out of your month.
- Make a hard copy list of the content that you have already memorised. Do it over a period of weeks. Include, for arguments sake, oddities of information that you've never entirely forgotten from your youth and any areas you 'half know' that could be patched up.
- Pick a root for your memory palace.
- Start. Waiting for a perfect structure is the same as having no structure.
- Let me know how you get on.

# Bibliography

[Brown, 2007] Brown, D. (2007). *Tricks of the Mind.* Channel 4.

[Caplan and Winterbottom, 2016] Caplan, H. and Winterbottom, M. (2016). Rhetorica ad herennium (the translation, obviously). In *Oxford Research Encyclopedia of Classics.*

[Cleveland et al., 2017] Cleveland, W., Alvarez, M., and Nation, T. (2017). *Yo Millard Fillmore! (And all those other Presidents you don't know).* Easton Studio Press, LLC.

[Cooke, 2008] Cooke, E. (2008). *Remember, Remember: Learn the Stuff You Thought You Never Could.* Penguin Adult.

[Einstein and McDaniel, 1987] Einstein, G. O. and McDaniel, M. A. (1987). *Distinctiveness and the Mnemonic Benefits of Bizarre Imagery*, pages 78–102. Springer New York, New York, NY.

[Foer, 2012] Foer, J. (2012). *Moonwalking with Einstein: The Art and Science of Remembering Everything.* Penguin science. Penguin.

[Harris, 2018] Harris, T. (2018). *Hannibal: (Hannibal Lecter).* Hannibal Lecter. Random House.

[Higbee, 2001] Higbee, K. (2001). *Your Memory: How it Works and how to Improve it.* Marlowe & Company.

[Kahn, ] Kahn, B. The longest dewey decimal number. `https://oeis.org/A242782/internal`.

[Legge et al., 2012] Legge, E. L., Madan, C. R., Ng, E. T., and Caplan, J. B. (2012). Building a memory palace in minutes: Equivalent memory performance using virtual versus conventional environments with the method of loci. *Acta psychologica*, 141(3):380–390.

[Lorayne, 1958] Lorayne, H. (1958). *How to Develop a Super Power Memory.* Thorsons.

[Losh, 2013] Losh, S. (2013). *Learn Vimscript the Hard way.* Steve Losh.

[Luriia et al., 1987] Luriia, A., Bruner, J., and Solotaroff, L. (1987). *The Mind of a Mnemonist: A Little Book about a Vast Memory.* Harvard University Press.

[Marbas and Pelley, 2002] Marbas, L. and Pelley, J. (2002). *Visual Mnemonics for Microbiology and Immunology.* Visual mnemonics series. Blackwell Science.

[Massen et al., 2009] Massen, C., Vaterrodt-Plünnecke, B., Krings, L., and Hilbig, B. E. (2009). Effects of instruction on learners ability to generate an effective pathway in the method of loci. *Memory*, 17(7):724–731.

[McDaniel et al., 1995] McDaniel, M. A., Einstein, G. O., DeLosh, E. L., May, C. P., and Brady, P. (1995). The bizarreness effect: It's not surprising, it's complex. *Journal of Experimental Psychology: Learning, Memory, and Cognition*, 21(2):422.

[Midttun, 2016] Midttun, S. (2016). *Mnemonics Memory Palace*. How to Build a Memory Palace. CreateSpace Independent Publishing Platform.

[O'Brien, 2016] O'Brien, D. (2016). *You Can Have an Amazing Memory: Learn Life-changing Techniques and Tips from the Memory Maestro*. Watkins Media Limited.

[Pugh, 1990] Pugh, W. (1990). Skip lists: a probabilistic alternative to balanced trees. *Communications of the ACM*, 33(6):668–676.

[Rees, 2012] Rees, T. (2012). Hacking scrabble. `https://teajaymars.com/post/hacking-scrabble-part-2`.

[Richman, 1994] Richman, C. L. (1994). The bizarreness effect with complex sentences: Temporal effects. *Canadian Journal of Experimental Psychology/Revue canadienne de psychologie expérimentale*, 48(3):444.

[Riefer and Rouder, 1992] Riefer, D. M. and Rouder, J. N. (1992). A multinomial modeling analysis of the mnemonic benefits of bizarre imagery. *Memory & Cognition*, 20(6):601–611.

[Singhal and Singhal, 2015] Singhal, A. and Singhal, S. (2015). *How to Memorize Anything: The Ultimate Handbook to Explore and Improve Your Memory.* Random House Publishers India Pvt. Limited.

[Skiena, 2009] Skiena, S. (2009). *The Algorithm Design Manual.* Springer London.

[Spence, 2008] Spence, J. (2008). *The Memory Palace of Matteo Ricci.* Quercus.

[Wikipedia, 2020] Wikipedia (2020). The family tree of Sigmund Christoph von Waldburg-Zeil-trauchburg.

[Wikipedia, 2020a] Wikipedia (2020a). Howard brown (halifax bank). `https://en.wikipedia.org/wiki/Howard_Brown_(Halifax_Bank)`.

[Wikipedia, 2020b] Wikipedia (2020b). List of world heritage sites in the united kingdom. `https://en.wikipedia.org/wiki/List_of_World_Heritage_Sites_in_the_United_Kingdom`.

[Wiseman, 2018] Wiseman, R. (2018). *How to Remember Everything.* Quercus.

[Yates, 1992] Yates, F. A. (1992). *The Art of Memory*, volume 64. Random House.

[Yousaf, 2006] Yousaf, S. (2006). *Mnemonics for Medical Undergraduates*. PasTest.

# Index

Made in the USA
Las Vegas, NV
11 April 2025

20837341R00115